The Intentional Apartment Developer

Advanced Praise

●

"Apartment supply is important for our country. Derek Lobo has assembled a resource that aims to help developers in their efforts to pivot to apartment development."

Mark Kenney
President and CEO
CAPREIT

"I wish I had this book before I built my first apartment, but I had access to the author, and he's guided me through multiple successful apartment developments."

Rob Piroli
President
Piroli Construction

"I have known Derek since he launched his first business in 1986. Over these 35 years, he has earned a reputation as the "go-to apartment expert" in Canada. *The Intentional Apartment Developer* is a compilation of decades of his know-how and will definitely be helpful to apartment developers and the real estate fraternity."

George Przybylowski
Vice President, Real Estate
Informa Canada

"*The Intentional Apartment Developer* is a complete guide to all the topics needed to be considered when developing an apartment building. In this big puzzle with moving parts, Derek and his team helped us ask the right questions and make quality decisions."

Oren Vered
President
Vared Group

Other Books by Derek Lobo

The Future Apartment Developer: The Blueprint for Building Rental Apartments and Intergenerational Wealth (MPS-Dala, 2021)

A *Field Guide to Rental Apartment Development by the Numbers: Building and Testing a Detailed Financial Feasibility Model* (MPS-Dala, 2021)

The Feasibility Study Determines the Apartment You Build: How to Build the Right Apartment Building in the Right Location for the Right Resident (MPS-Dala, 2021)

Finding Money to Build Apartments: Make Better Deals by Finding Cheaper Capital (MPS-Dala, 2021)

A Field Guide to Municipal Taxes and Operating Costs: Decreasing Your Operating Costs to Maximize Value (MPS-Dala, 2021)

The Four Factors That Drive Rent: Why $100 More in Rent = $24,000 in Increased Value (MPS-Dala, 2021)

Intensifying Existing Developments with Apartments: Apartments Are the Most Profitable Additions When Intensifying Land (MPS-Dala, 2021)

Building Apartments With a Joint Venture Partner: Structuring a Deal so That the Lender, Developer, and Partner Win (MPS-Dala, 2021)

Writing and Executing the Marketing Plan: Strategies to Get Your Building Full at the Highest Rent (MPS-Dala, 2021)

Writing and Executing a Sales and Leasing Plan: Hiring, Training, Managing, and Compensating Your Leasing Staff for Maximum Results (MPS-Dala, 2021)

Designing Apartments for the Future: Meeting Modern Expectations With Innovative Design (MPS-Dala, 2021)

Becoming a Successful Merchant Apartment Builder: Developing a Business Plan and Growing Your Wealth (MPS-Dala, 2021)

Finding and Acquiring Land for Apartment Development: Processes for Site Selection Through Closing (MPS-Dala, 2021)

A Private Developer's Roadmap for Affordable Housing: Profitable Rental Apartment Solutions in Canada (Dala, 2022)

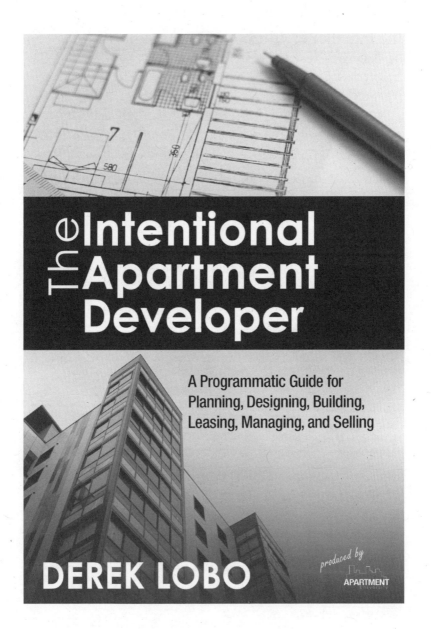

The Intentional Apartment Developer

A Programmatic Guide for Planning, Designing, Building, Leasing, Managing, and Selling

DEREK LOBO

produced by
APARTMENT University

DALA™
Derek A. Lobo & Associates
Group of Companies

The Intentional Apartment Developer

Derek Lobo

Produced by Apartment University

Published by DALA Inc.
TM and Copyright ©2022 Derek Lobo

Derek Lobo
Apartment University
905-331-5700
derek@derek-lobo.com
derek.lobo@rockadvisorsinc.com

ISBN: 978-1-7773648-3-0 (hardcover)
            978-1-7773648-5-4 (eBook)

Printed in Canada
First Edition, May 2022

Editor: Rory d'Eon
Contributing Editor: Darryl McCullough
Proofreading: Geri Savits-Fine
Interior Layout: Rod Schulhauser, Adam Carter
Cover: Rod Schulhauser
Project Management: Rod Schulhauser & DALA Inc.

Dedication

I dedicate this book to all the courageous men and women
who put it all on the line to build rental apartments.

These people are my heroes!

DEREK
LOBO

Table Of Contents

List of Figures

Before We Get Started...

First of all, thank you for getting your eyes on the pages of this book! My promise to you is that it will be worth your time to digest the decades of knowledge that I have assembled here.

Something For You

Before we dive in, I want to give you a gift that I do not share anywhere else. It's a business tool that has shaped the way I execute projects of all sizes, prepare for important calls, strategize for vital negotiations, and develop vision for future endeavors. Rarely a day goes by where I don't use this strategy, either by myself or with team members. It's about selling myself on an idea first before taking action or pitching it.

You will find your gift here:

 strategiccoach.com/go/impactfilter_tiad

This **Impact Filter** has enabled me to become intentional with my efforts, forces me to be patient rather than react, and ultimately gives me focus and clarity so that I act with specific intent.

Enjoy!

Setting the Stage

Next, I want to share some concepts that will set the stage for your journey forward so you can better understand my mindset and motivation. My success in business is all about providing an **Apartment Development FULL Service Experience**™. This consists of two key ingredients:

1. Being available
2. Adding value

Being available is accomplished by "staying in traffic" (a term I often use) and remaining easy to connect with. **Adding value** is the glue that creates a mutually beneficial relationship and keeps clients coming back to the experience you provide them.

Apartment Intelligence and Leadership is our motto, and we do this through seven essential elements. We'll cover these in more detail later.

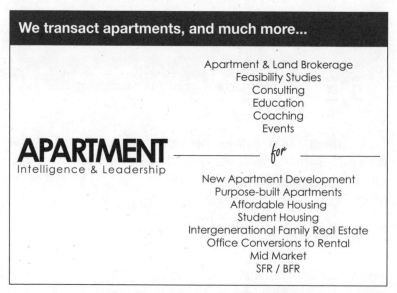

We transact apartments, and much more...

Apartment & Land Brokerage
Feasibility Studies
Consulting
Education
Coaching
Events

APARTMENT
Intelligence & Leadership

for

New Apartment Development
Purpose-built Apartments
Affordable Housing
Student Housing
Intergenerational Family Real Estate
Office Conversions to Rental
Mid Market
SFR / BFR

Figure 0.1 - Rock Advisors - What We Do

I value and appreciate the success I have realized to date and continue to create for others. Our team is filled with like-minded individuals who are focused on our niche industry. Most prototypical brokerage firms are broad in scope and narrow in providing a unique client experience. From the outset, I have been laser-focused on the apartment industry. Today, we have in-house capabilities that include research, underwriting, lease-up, custom content creation, marketing asset production, publishing, interactive webinars, live-event production, and brokerage.

What do I mean by an **Apartment Development FULL Service Experience**™? It is a beginning-to-end process—from the inception of the new apartment construction project, all the way to the end—which could be the setup of ongoing asset management or the sale of the asset.

Figure 0.2 - Apartment Development FULL Service Experience™

This **Apartment Development FULL Service Experience**™ was designed for three important reasons:
1. Help you make more money
2. Arm you with insight to avoid pitfalls that cause developers to lose money
3. Bring together resources to execute best practices

If you're reading this and perhaps thinking, "This guy is just selling me his business," you're right. But here's the real message I want you to take away: at the end of the day, you can gain your experience by learning from your own mistakes and victories, *or* you can leverage the wisdom of decades of hands-on knowledge, strategy, and tactics, and immediately deploy that wisdom and knowledge on your very first (or next) project! There is no need to wait while you learn from your mistakes and develop your personal experiences.

Like many other businesses, apartment development success is greatly enhanced by "who you know," which relates back to my earlier statement about "bringing together resources to execute best practices." My business has flourished because of long-lasting, intergenerational, and mutually beneficial relationships, which is the result of working with clients from the early stages of their vision all the way through to completion and/or sale.

Collaboration is key. I have learned from my mentors that sometimes perceived competitors can be ideal collaborators when you both share the same "hero." What's important to note is that collaboration doesn't involve the exchange of money. When combining resources and talent, powerful results can be attained by working with others to achieve a common purpose and serve the same end-client. I love to collaborate, and it has yielded many opportunities and benefits!

Learning On Demand

One more item before we get started, and I've saved the best for last. I am personally excited for the future-based focus we've developed. Part of that focus has resulted in the creation of our new online learning portal, *Apartment University*, which can be found at derek-lobo.com. This project is the result of assembling our collected amortized knowledge and presenting it in a skills-on-demand and lifelong learning platform. Learning has been siloed for such a long time, but today we have the technology to multiply the educational experience for anyone.

We have deployed a modern Content Management System (CMS), also known as a Learning Management System (LMS), and assembled an industry-first tool that is invaluable to the aspiring apartment developer. This learning portal is aimed specifically at the needs of new apartment developers, developers who are pivoting to apartments, affordable and student-housing developers, and many other sectors that support the apartment development process (research, financing, marketing, leasing, staff development, etc.). These needs are filled and delivered through:

- Courses
- Videos
- Interviews
- eBooks
- Business tools
- Webinars
- Events
- Coaching
- Skill development
- Industry strategy and insight

I personally want to invite you to explore *Apartment University*. Check it out for free and explore this resource—there's no other like it anywhere!

Figure 0.3 - Apartment University Learning Portal

Starting the Journey

I want to be your ROCK ADVISOR: a solid voice of wisdom, strategy, and focus. I appreciate the time you are dedicating to absorb this book. Dig into these pages—mark them up, dog-ear the corners, highlight key points that resonate with you, and extract the value contained within. And don't forget to claim your free gift, which I shared earlier.

To begin this journey together, I invite you to turn the page and take the path, step-by-step, through *The Intentional Apartment Developer*.

Acknowledgements

A project, such as this, does not happen on its own or without the collective efforts of a team of like-minded, focused people! With that in mind, I need to thank those who've been directly and indirectly involved in the creation of this endeavor.

It all starts with our Rock Advisors team, who pull together the content, expertise, knowledge, relationships, and skills to make my vision a reality. They are the gears of the machine that creates, markets, and sells.

Of course, none of this would matter if it weren't for our clients and collaborators! They are the visionaries of the apartment development industry, and I am eternally thankful for their business, trust, and friendship.

I also wish to extend my appreciation to Dan Sullivan, whose mentorship and friendship have been pivotal in shaping my strategic thinking and opening new avenues for me to explore both at work and at home.

Thank you all!

Foreword

News of the scarcity of rental housing has never been more prominent—for good reason. Rental housing is crucial for many people in our society: immigrants, young people, families, foreign students, and seniors. It's vital to serve these groups for the well-being of society and our country. Our economy cannot grow if there is an absence of affordable housing. According to a 2018 Statistics Canada survey (150.statcan.gc.ca/t1/tbl1/en/tv.action?pid=1110000801), 73 percent of the Canadian population earns less than $50,000 before taxes. As some of the nation's largest rental housing providers, we believe that supply is the key to a healthy and sustainable rental market.

For more than three decades, we have seen Derek become a leader in the apartment industry, and an advocate of new apartment development. *The Intentional Apartment Developer* is a road map for becoming an apartment developer.

This book serves as a guide for developers who want to build rental apartments. If you're an experienced developer, there are many valuable lessons contained in this book. If you're new or pivoting to apartments, this book is for you.

Our wish for you, the intentional apartment developer, is to fully embrace the social and economic significance of this important and impactful journey.

Mark Kenney
President and CEO
CAPREIT

Bob Dhillon
President and CEO
Mainstreet Equity Corp

Philip Fraser
President and CEO
Killam Apartment REIT

Overview

Historically, multifamily development has been the best opportunity for a developer seeking both short-term capital gains and longer-term wealth creation. With the information in this text, developers—especially first-time developers—can take full advantage of this opportunity.

We have assembled a comprehensive suite of resources: the original *Apartment Developer University* webinar series, the *Apartment Developer University* 13-book series, and the resources available at our learning portal: *Apartment University* at derek-lobo.com. Together, they help equip multifamily developers with the necessary knowledge, advice, skills, and proven processes to successfully compete in the marketplace.

These resources will change, or add to, a developer's perspective on building apartments, enabling them to confidently serve their customers and become successful programmatic (according to a program or defined method) builders.

The Hero Builder

We've always been fascinated by the first-time apartment developer who one day risks everything to develop a specific piece of land to fulfill a vision. That individual commits financial resources, personal covenant, and a huge investment in time to build a multifamily development. It is, however, that first apartment building that opens up an opportunity to grow into a successful merchant apartment builder.

The Intentional Apartment Developer is about this hero. It's about creating a bigger, better, more exciting future, with reliable, actionable strategies that lead to successful development.

Our Mission

Typically, a developer who has experience in other asset classes has 90 percent of the skills needed to become a successful apartment builder. Our mission is to enable that developer to access the key remaining 10 percent. We can teach the developer how to think, communicate, take action, achieve results, and pivot existing skills into becoming a successful, vertically integrated builder.

This book is specifically targeted to new apartment developers, their staff, and the commercial real estate fraternity that supports them. We have a team of dedicated professionals who can facilitate planning, feasibility, financing, design, and ultimate disposition of apartments. By becoming a well-informed apartment developer, it is possible to leave behind the competition of the cyclical asset classes and enter an in-demand asset class where the wealth stays with the developer and the business for years to come.

Figure 0.4 - A Developer of Developers - It's Who We Are

The "why" behind building apartments always comes back to the developer's family and legacy. It's about wealth preservation, tax deferral, and cash flow. And the reason this all works is that rentals are the best way for a real estate family to transition wealth from one generation to another.

We want developers, their families, and future generations to enjoy the fruits of sound financial planning to enable a smooth transfer of their hard-earned assets for a bigger and more exciting future.

The Fundamentals of Success

The following chapters introduce developers to the principles and fundamentals necessary to begin, develop, lease-up, and sell or keep a viable project. We encourage developers to explore our learning portal for in-depth presentations of pertinent topics led by leading industry experts. It also is a chance to meet other developers just like you.

derek-lobo.com APARTMENT University The Apartment Development ONLINE LEARNING PLATFORM

In our experience, developers love meeting other developers. Our conferences and field trips provide developers the opportunity to share experiences and common best practices in a stress-free, supportive atmosphere. Along with our other resources, such events prepare developers to build confidently, face challenges successfully, avoid the pitfalls that may cause them to lose money, and ultimately, complete projects that meet the developer's original financial and personal objectives.

Introduction

●

This book contains a wealth of information. It's a compilation of over 30 years of amortized knowledge solely focused on building wealth through apartment development. By combining those years of experience with our proven, unique processes and dedicated teams of professionals, a developer can take advantage of an asset class that has long-term stability and profitability, and be on the way to building a successful, wealth-generating business. We strive to fully inform the developer so they become an "apartment scientist." With our teams taking care of the details, they're free to focus on building a business that programmatically builds successful rental apartments time and time again.

Our Apartment Development FULL Service Experience™

This book is really our Apartment Development FULL Service Experience™, beginning with an apartment's conception to either its final sale or long-term ownership, and organized into distinct stages that are easy to understand.

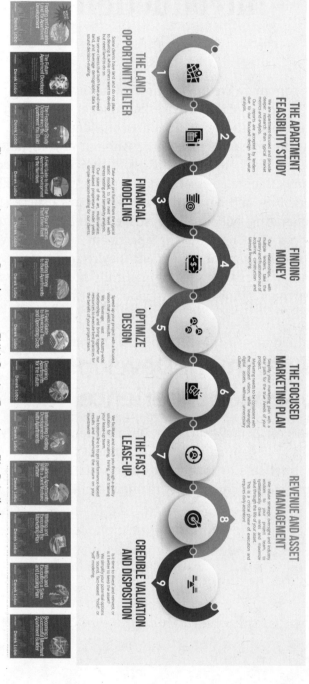

Apartment Development
FULL Service Experience™

THE APARTMENT FEASIBILITY STUDY
We are apartment focused and provide deeper research than typical market metrics and analysis.
Our reports are accepted by lenders due to our focused design and value analysis.

THE LAND OPPORTUNITY FILTER
Some clients have land and do not plan to develop it, while others want to develop but need land to do so.
We serve clients that both have and need land, and leverage demographic data for sound decision-making.

FINDING MONEY
Our relationships with multiple lenders take the mystery and frustration out of acquiring construction and seed financing.

FINANCIAL MODELING
Take your pro forma from the typical static model, to the next level with stress testing and sensitivity analysis.
Our state of the art, multi-variate, time-based proprietary model yields simple decision-making for our clients.

THE FOCUSED MARKETING PLAN
Simplify your marketing plan with a clear path for the true needs of your project.
Marketing needs to be consistent with the focused vision, while leveraging digital assets, without unnecessary clutter.

OPTIMIZE DESIGN
Speed up your project with a focused vision that yields results.
We leverage industry-wide relationships and bring together our resources to execute best practices for the benefit of your project team.

REVENUE AND ASSET MANAGEMENT
We utilize strategic oversight and industry wisdom to your project team to systematically drive revenue and maximize value through the life of your asset.
This is a critical phase of execution and requires daily attention!

THE FAST LEASE-UP
We facilitate and coach you through a quality solution for your lease-up team.
The bottom line is to get performance-based results, and maximizing the return on your investment.

CREDIBLE VALUATION AND DISPOSITION
Is it time to divest and reinvest, or is it better to keep the asset?
We simplify your potential options with sound, fact-based "hold" or "sell" modeling.

Figure 0.5 - Apartment Development FULL Service Experience™ - Detailed

Our relationship with the developer begins early in the process. Often, we are one of the first professionals they engage. Our goal is to determine whether a potential project can be developed into a profitable investment. We evaluate where they can expect the highest rents, where demand is highest, and where municipal taxes are lowest. We then proceed to an opportunity study, using in-depth demographic and economic data to help pinpoint the best opportunities.

From there, we prepare a project feasibility study. Many times, it's at this stage that developers come to us. They may already own a piece of desirable land or wish to buy one, but aren't quite sure how, or if, to proceed.

It's at this point we can provide the clarity needed for decision-making. If based on our experience we don't think a deal is viable, it's a free, fast "no." If we think a project is viable, then the developer should proceed with a financial feasibility study, which will show how the deal pencils out using a variety of metrics such as development yield and initial rate of return (IRR). Later, we can arrange for a joint venture (JV) partner. In our experience, most developers know how to get construction financing, but finding mezzanine and equity financing (when needed) is a bigger challenge. If needed, we will connect developers with potential mezzanine and equity financing partners.

Working with the design team, architects, landscapers, and interior designers comes next to ensure the developer is designing a building that will get them the highest rent possible. Many of the decisions such professionals make are based on our feasibility study. Since we know what the resident profile looks like—whether it be young urban professionals, affluent seniors, or singles—design decisions based on the potential renters' needs can be made.

At this point, actual construction begins. While that proceeds, we will continue to write and execute a thorough marketing plan, which began when the hoarding went up. We compile a priority waiting list—that part is vital. Once the marketing plan is done, we'll begin the initial lease-up phase. That means hiring, training, and managing the staff for the actual lease-up after certificate of occupancy.

Developers who hold on to their buildings often decide to continue working with us on a consulting basis to help manage their properties. That usually means advice on rental rates and taking steps to minimize turnover. If the developer is a merchant builder, we may proceed to the broker stage and sell the building.

Why Apartments?

Why not focus on retail or single-family homes? Isn't that where the traditional money is made? To get to these answers, we must look at the big picture.

The dot-com bubble (and consequent bursting), the financial crisis of 2008, and the COVID-19 pandemic caused much uncertainty in rental markets. However, apartments have historically been decoupled from the ebb and flow of economic cycles. Rental apartments are often the first sector to recover after an economic downturn—this was the case following the 2008 financial crisis. Today, if we look closely at rental market conditions, we'll see that the underlying factors are still very favorable. In short, rental markets have a very bright future.

Over the past decade, new A-Class (top of the market) buildings have created a sweet spot. From the investors' point of view, investors and pension funds have money available and are underweighted in rental apartment buildings. They've come to realize that apartments are a stable asset class, despite changing economic conditions.

What If You're a Renter?

Across North America, there's a shortage of high-quality rental units (in some areas). From the renters' perspective, it means they must wait longer and pay more. We don't see this situation changing anytime soon.

In many markets, changing demographics and rising homeownership prices often create conditions where consumers look into high quality rental options over home purchases. We think that this will drive the rise of the rental market, further informing developers that their number one priority as entrepreneurs should be to seek out those opportunities and capitalize on them.

The Apartment Builder's Legacy

Institutional investors do not want to buy buildings designed and built in the 1950s, 60s or 70s. None of these are buildings that current renters want to live in. Buyers and renters are looking for up-to-date apartments, which look like high-end office buildings on the outside and condominiums on the inside. Apartments built this way command the highest rent, the highest net operating income (NOI), and lowest cap rate.

In addition, interest rates have been at an all-time low for the past few years and are likely to remain low into the foreseeable future. This means there are financiers ready, willing, and able to invest in new buildings and developments—we just need the developers to build them.

A Perfect Storm

Let's put all this information into perspective. We know the single biggest expense when developing an apartment is the cost of capital. Over the past few years, financing costs have been at an all-time low, quality renters are plentiful, and financiers have money.

 Together, this has created a perfect storm.

Becoming an Apartment Scientist

Our company's mission is to help developers gain the confidence to proceed to a successful project. Apartment development has a long, bright future. With our help, condominium, industrial property, hotel, and shopping center developers can position themselves as programmatic builders. This opens up an opportunity to create a new business within an existing one that will protect their wealth, create a steady stream of cash flow, and defer taxes through depreciation.

Start with the End in Mind

In anticipation of building and keeping (at least some) of the apartments built by a developer, we coach their estate for an efficient transfer of assets to the next generation. If they'd rather become a merchant builder, we want them to think about their legacy. (Merchant builders, also referred to as merchant developers, are those developers who build properties and sell them rather than holding on to such properties for extended periods.)

We have created our process so that the aspiring developer can become a successful apartment developer/owner or a successful merchant builder. We've been able to do so based on decades of relationships, hands-on experience, writing books/publications, executing seminars/events, and our business process that connects developers with competent industry resources and experts.

Take a moment to think about the home-building market of the 1960s and 70s. Most cannot name any of the builders from that time. However, these businesses are mostly still around and active in the industry. The companies that have been passed on to children and grandchildren are all benefiting from a stable, rental income because rental buildings are all about wealth creation, not short-term business income. As a result, those buildings have become the builder's legacy.

Apartment buildings build wealth.

Changing a builder's focus from short-term income to long-term income is not difficult. Once apprised of the knowledge contained in the *Apartment Developer University* book series (which is now part of our learning portal) and resources available through the *Apartment University* learning portal, builders will see the proposition of building rental apartments in a different light. They'll now have an opportunity to accumulate the know-how needed to take advantage of this asset class in the pursuit of their long-term financial and personal goals.

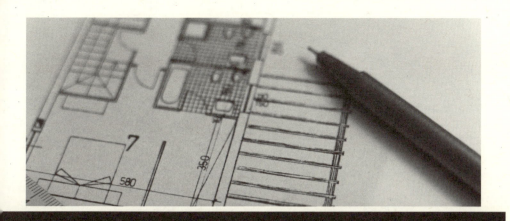

PART 1: What to Build

The Feasibility Study

Broadly speaking, a feasibility study is a technique used to assess a project's viability before the investment of invaluable time and resources. The aim is to objectively evaluate the strengths, weaknesses, opportunities, and threats of a proposed purpose-built rental project, whether it be through a sole developer or a joint venture partnership. The study provides the developer or development group, and potential investors, with the confidence that they're building the most profitable project for their specific site. The assessment is built on detailed demographic and economic analysis, combined with rental comparables. Ultimately, the most profitable building to develop will be the one that best meets the renters' needs. Though the developer's opinion is valuable, the overriding factor is where the data is leading them.

A feasibility study is the foundation of a successful project.

A feasibility study serves two different purposes. First, it's needed for internal decision-making. Without a good grasp of the market, and the financials and potential outcomes, solid decision-making is next to impossible. Second, investors and lenders will demand a detailed study to assure themselves that the developer has thought the project through adequately and knows deep down that the project is viable and has sound data to back up those claims.

For a developer considering whether to build or not, the study answers five crucial questions:

1. Should they build?
2. What should they build?
3. What is the depth of the market?
4. How much rent can they charge?
5. How much will their building be worth after they build in order to either sell or refinance?

Once those answers are available, developers stand a much better chance of reaching their intended goals.

Should You Build?

For more on where you might build, see Chapter 5: Finding and Acquiring Land

What Makes a Good Rental Site?

Four factors drive rent: location, unit mix and sizing, amenities, and the property management platform.

While a developer can't change your location, they can choose to develop in a site that naturally appeals to renters. Renters aged 40 to over 50 desire close proximity to employment and walking trails. They are typically less concerned with transit connections and rely on local and regional highway connections to commute. Many of these renters are downsizing and well into their established careers. They want access to commercial retailers and they don't want to increase commuting time, which means good highway access—plus they like eating out at restaurants.

Although interior amenities are important, community amenities are equally as important. A building doesn't exist in a vacuum, and neither do residents. The community amenities are what an individual is likely to require day-to-day. The closer these amenities are to the site, the stronger the site becomes for rental development. Community amenities include such things as availability of transit, parks, green space and outdoor recreational facilities, shopping, and health-care facilities.

A target renter will also desire specific social amenities. For example, young professionals want a varied and exciting nightlife, like bars, pubs, clubs, and theater. Also, since they commute to work, they need access to good transit. Though many seniors and retirees remain in the workforce, a majority are retired and do not commute daily. They're more concerned with having their daily conveniences within walking distance—amenities like cafés, restaurants, and parks—and having access to health-care services such as hospitals and pharmacies. This might sound a bit cliché, but ultimately when we study the reasons why older people downsize into apartments, we find that when they live in close proximity to those services, they're more comfortable.

Normally, when considering a new development, the developer is not targeting families. How can they expect a family to pay top-of-market rent for a two-bedroom apartment when that same amount will allow them to rent a house in a secondary market? Lower-density products in secondary and tertiary markets are better suited for children and families. These families also need sports facilities and schools, which are not something found in dense urban environments.

Understanding the Different Markets

There are five distinct markets: urban (city downtown), suburban/urban (outside of downtown but with significant development), suburban (cities near a large urban area), secondary (cities at a distance from large urban areas), and tertiary (small towns).

Development profit varies between those markets. A downtown (urban) high-rise has the lowest development yield, a suburban/urban mid-rise has a higher yield, and a low-rise in a suburban location has the highest yield.

Urban Versus Suburban Renters

The young downtown urban renter sleeps in the apartment but lives in the building and neighborhood, whereas suburban renters live in the streets and play in their units (that is, they use the streets to drive places, but their home is where they spend their leisure time). By suburban renters, we also mean renters in secondary and tertiary markets.

Normally, smaller units are built in urban markets, the unit sizes growing as one moves outside of the downtown core. There, neighborhood amenities are scarcer, and residents spend more time indoors as those communities have fewer local amenities.

Secondary and Tertiary Markets

Secondary and tertiary markets typically refer to suburban communities or municipalities that surround major markets.

Tertiary markets are typically smaller communities, many of which are towns some distance from larger urban centers. Because of their size, planning and zoning usually takes less time. These municipalities generally don't have the backlog that busier primary markets do. In addition, developers have more direct relationships with municipal planners, making negotiations easier. In combination, this makes development very attractive.

Markets and Demand

Downtown sites have a proven market and demand, making financing easier to arrange. Incomes are generally higher with a greater percentage of renters versus those who will (or have) bought. However, competition for renters is intense. Land prices are also high due to competing developers and usage—whatever development may potentially offer the greatest return can achieve the greatest land value—especially in some specific local areas.

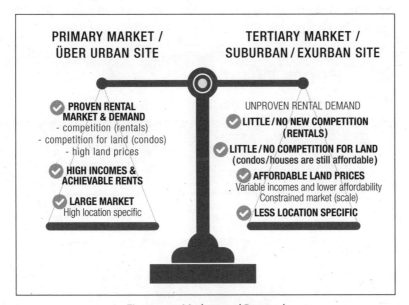

Figure 1.1 - Markets and Demand

In secondary and tertiary markets, demand for rental is often unproven, which means an extensive study to prove the existence of rental demand. Incomes are typically lower compared to a more urban location, with reduced affordability. However, this doesn't matter because land cost is lower, and a developer doesn't need to collect as much money per square foot to make a viable investment. Since the rental pool is smaller, a smaller development is adequate. And finally, since there is less new competition for renters, land and the specific location is less critical.

What Should You Build?

Once a developer has decided on a building's location, finding out what to build becomes the priority. The feasibility study's objective is to uncover the details of a specific development site that affect viability and profitability. These details are specific to that site: current market conditions, current investor interest, and current potential renter availability. A developer can now position their development, so it stands above the competition.

Who Rents What?

The first consideration is to identify who the target renters are. The way units are designed will be different based on the type of available renter.

UNIT TYPE	TARGET RENTER	
	Primary Market	Secondary & Tertiary Market
Bachelor	Students, shelter renters	AVOID
One Bedroom	25-35 y/o early career divorcees (minority), single downsizers	25-35 y/o early career divorcees, single downsizers
One Bedroom + Den	Roommates, divorcees, single downsizers	Divorcees, single downsizers
Two Bedrooms	Roommates, young couples (high income), older downsizers (minority)	Older downsizers, divorcees (high income), young couples (minority)
Two Bedrooms + Den	Roommates, older downsizers	Older downsizers, couples (minority)
Three Bedrooms	AVOID (but roommates)	AVOID (but older downsizers)

Figure 1.2 - Target Renters for Different Unit Types

Different renters have different priorities:
- Roommates want equity in bedroom size and bathroom access.
- Downsizers need storage, expect upgraded kitchens, and in-suite space to entertain.
- Younger residents need entertainment space as well but will consider common areas as a solution.
- Divorcees may want one-bedroom units plus a den.
- Families may want three-bedroom units.

The feasibility study will reveal the availability of each of these groups, along with household incomes, work and leisure habits, and age distribution. This makes unit design decisions easier.

Materials, Finishes, and Amenities

Material choice, finish level, and amenities can depend on whether you're keeping the building or selling it.

How much amenity space should be built?

Typically, we recommend between 15 and 25 square feet of functional interior amenity space be allocated per unit. Smaller buildings typically offer 20 to 25 square feet, while larger developments, which have the benefit of scale, can allocate between 15 and 20 square feet of amenity space per unit. Once this space is allocated, the developer needs to decide how it will be used and what proportion is ideal for each amenity.

Buildings developed with long-term holding in mind typically provide more amenities because the developer wants the building to remain competitive with other local comparable properties over a much longer time frame.

Buildings developed for sale compete with the immediate market. There's less concern with the long-term viability of the project. These properties are designed to compete with the existing market and what's in the development pipeline.

Please refer to Chapter 13, "The Big Question," for a more detailed look at the "build-to-hold or build-to-sell" question.

Phased Developments

Phased development makes sense under one of the following circumstances:

1. When the lot area allows for multiple buildings
2. When multiple buildings, leased over time, don't oversaturate the market

Though newer buildings compete with older ones, they also exist together, and because of their proximity, affect one another. The benefit is that amenities can be shared between the buildings, thereby maximizing rentable space.

What Is the Depth of the Market?

If a market is reaching saturation, lease-up and absorption will be affected. A simple way to understand the depth of a given market is to look at the number of apartments per 100 people.

RENTAL DENSITY = (RENTAL UNIVERSE / POPULATION) X 100

By adding the additional new units, a developer can determine the expected rental density and proximity to market saturation.

How Much Rent Can Be Charged?

A proposed project's competition can be established with a thorough market survey. We concentrate on A-Class products, such as a condominium and a new high-quality rental product, and B-Class products that have been renovated to an A-standard even if it's in a B-Class building.

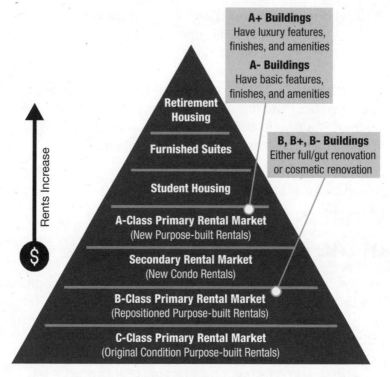

Figure 1.3 - Rental Rates Versus Building Class

In some markets, even by casting a wide net, developers often find they are building in a neighborhood with no direct competition. This is not an undesirable situation, but it makes it more challenging to predict what the optimum rents should be. Though they may be setting top-of-the-market rents, they need to balance their pro forma with what the market will bear.

Comparables

To get a basic idea what the rental market looks like, we review comparables. There are different types of comparables: new-in-the-market and older comparables.

New Comparables

Depending on the market, finding new rentals is fairly easy. If a building is in a secondary or tertiary market, direct comparables may be more difficult to find, necessitating the need to look further afield. For those, we search in other communities with the same demographics, income and population size, and competition.

Older Comparables

In markets with few comparable units, we rely on indirect market data. This means researching condo rentals and older, renovated buildings.

Other Considerations

In our experience, tenants will pay for superior management. A competent, responsive, well-trained management team will make that apartment the market leader and be able to set rents higher than comparables. If a developer is concerned with rent per square foot, they may miss the value inherent in the charm and individual characteristics of the unit (the value proposition of a unit)—that is, its features, finishes, views, and overall functionality.

Individual Unit Advantages

In some cases, a building with a high percentage of large units can actually perform better on an NOI basis than a building with many smaller units. Although there are fewer units overall, the rent collected per unit is higher. However, operating expenses are consistent and the overall NOI may experience an increase.

It pays to explore every avenue when setting a building's rents, including detailed unit analysis of every unit's pros and cons. Some unit details will enable higher rents, generating extra money month after month.

A Building's Value

The four key components of a building's value are:
- Rents
- Ancillary sources of income
- Operating expenses
- Cap rate

The ultimate end of a feasibility study is a project-wide operating pro forma. To this end, we're often asked to name the most important inputs. It's at this stage where first-time developers sometimes get it wrong: they're very good at land and construction costs but tend to "wing it" when it comes to setting rental rates. Further, they take a percentage of those (imprecise) rates to determine their operating costs. When doing that, they have just winged the foundation of their pro forma.

What the developer needs is line-by-line data—actual market data for rent and operating costs. Operating costs are not a percentage of income; they're line items in the budget the developer has researched. Setting market-maker rents is not only about what the building down the street is charging. A developer who designs a better building with amenities well matched to the intended target market can charge premium rents. Even if there are no direct competitors to base rents on, the opportunity to establish market-maker rents still does exist.

What really matters is the building's valuation and the return on investment (ROI), and how these feed into the developer's own financial portfolio and what they're trying to achieve. Once rents are set and operating expenses identified, developers can determine the building's valuation based on the property's NOI and an appropriate cap rate.

Conclusion

The feasibility study's role cannot be underestimated. Its value to a developer will not only be measured by higher renter satisfaction, but also in knowing they have built the best possible product for those renters. At the same time, they have realized as much value from their property as possible. We've seen too many developers build a product that they would like to live in rather than try to understand the type of product that renters actually *want* to live in.

The feasibility studies we conduct are a valuable investment— an insurance policy—to ensure that the building considered is viable and both fulfills the developer's goal to maximize value and brings to market an attractive rental product.

Stratford—Oxford Haus: A Sales Story

Challenge

Peter Hyde, born in Shakespeare just outside of Stratford, Ontario, was a local developer who wanted to build rental apartments in Stratford. He had remediated a former business site and built office space on one portion, and he wanted apartments on the remainder. However, there was no proof of concept. He didn't know if Stratford, a community of 30,000, could absorb a four-building, 236-unit development.

The challenge for us was to determine five things: one, should he build; two, what should he build; three, how much would he be able to charge for the units; four, what was the depth of the local market; and finally, what would the building be worth after it was built.

Action

We did our standard feasibility study, which revealed that without doubt, Stratford could absorb 236 units and he could charge enough rent to make a very good rate of return. Of course, this was only a report, so far. Further, Hyde had to be convinced. Over several meetings going over the details in the report, combined with our experience in apartment development, Hyde gained the confidence to begin building the four, 59-unit buildings.

Our next goal was to find capital. After the first building was built and leased, we brought in a buyer. They liked the project and they liked Hyde, but they were not convinced that Stratford could support all the extra units at equally high rents.

Hyde, still optimistic, built building two, which leased much faster with even stronger rents. We had proof that the concept did work. At that point, we brought the buyer—a major Canadian apartment owner—in again.

Based on the results of the first two buildings, they agreed to buy buildings three and four.

Result

There's a high degree of predictability of rent and absorption based on studying a city, its economics and demographics, and the persona of the resident profile. We knew, for instance, that in Stratford the majority of renters would be older.

We built larger units to suit their needs. We also built a separate clubhouse designed to give the residents a place to gather socially and hold functions—anything that needed extra space and amenities.

By reading the market accurately, we built a building designed for that market and the residents who lived there. Peter Hyde's development proved that there is a demand for apartments in small centers like Stratford.

Testimonial: Peter Hyde, Hyde Construction Ltd.

 I felt there was a great opportunity in Stratford, but I needed it well defined by a credible third party. When I was first introduced to Derek, we already knew that he understood the business I wanted to get into and he could provide the confidence we needed to proceed.

The feasibility study he produced helped us convince ourselves that there was indeed a viable opportunity there. Also, when we needed financing, we brought that same report to the lenders.

His team was there throughout development and lease-up, bringing credible buyers to the table. One of them bought the development—a buyer we have since developed a great relationship with.

Derek and his team's ability to offer a full service resulted in a better and more profitable project being built.

I highly recommend that any apartment developer involve them from the very beginning and keep them right through to the very end. Involving him and his team worked extremely well for us.

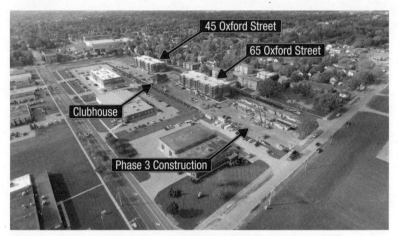

Figure 1.4 - Stratford - Oxford Haus

Rental Apartments by the Numbers

Introduction

The decision to move ahead with a development is all about a project's numbers. To understand them fully, it is important to build a detailed financial model. Once built, this does two things. One, if the numbers indicate that a project is not viable, it prevents a developer from moving ahead with a project that won't fulfill their goals. Two, it prevents a developer from abandoning what might be a profitable project.

The cost of developing a detailed financial model far outweighs the costs of actually developing a site, and then later, finding out that the financial picture is not satisfactory or that a valuable opportunity has been missed.

Nearly every project decision, from beginning to end, is impacted by those numbers.

The unique advantage we offer our clients is our 30+ years of experience combined with our unique knowledge and successful processes, which means we can predict profitability far more clearly. We have created and refined a detailed financial model that serves as a working pro forma specifically tailored to a purpose-built rental building. This allows developers to build a financial model able to pull in all the key variables into one easy-to-use system.

Once built and calibrated, design decisions can be made with authority and confidence. This enables a developer to run a sensitivity analysis on multiple project options and determine financial viability in the face of rising costs and changing fiscal conditions.

This model is especially valuable to newer or smaller developers who haven't had the time or resources to develop their own financial model. It's meant to give them the tools normally not available so that they are as informed as possible when making difficult and complex investment decisions.

Taming the Numbers

Building a financial model involves identifying all relevant costs associated with developing the property, including but not limited to hard costs, soft costs, and development charges. In addition, a full review of market conditions provides metrics such as cap rates, standard operating costs, and market rents.

The financial model then combines these factors in order to ascertain the financial viability of the subject development and overall estimated valuation.

We help the developer in providing the basic inputs, such as high-level unit mix and sizing, market rents, operating expenses, project timelines, and hard and soft costs. They must also input a series of front-end values, including but not limited to operating expenses and ancillary sources of income (parking charges, storage lockers, retail components, net metering, etc.). Back-end values include all associated hard and soft costs, costs of financing, and the timeline of the project, including pre-construction, construction, lease-up, and stabilization.

The developer must also identify additional lending assumptions, such as the term of their loan, loan amount, and interest rates. The developer is also responsible for collecting these assumptions from their various consultants, engineers, and cost estimators. As the development process progresses, they can continuously refine and update the model to accurately reflect the state of a development at any given time.

Building the Model

Base Case, Best Case, Worst Case

We begin with a basic set of assumptions that represent the current expected development scenario:

- The Base Case assumes the following: there are no significant construction or leasing delays and the project can be completed on or near schedule.
- The Best Case assumes the following: the developer gets preferential rates from their lender, construction times could be accelerated, lease-up is more efficient, operating expenses are reduced, and they achieve a lower cap rate than initially projected. This scenario, while unlikely, represents the best case that a developer could theoretically achieve if everything fell into place perfectly.

- The Worst Case anticipates cost overruns, interest rates on construction loans that are higher than initially expected, cost increases, prolonged timelines, and overall reduced returns. Though not a pleasant series of events, any of these must be planned for.

The Base Case Schedule

As in most developments, our base case development schedule covers a number of years. Not to state the obvious but building an apartment doesn't mean that everything begins at once. It does mean, however, that different parts of the project must begin when the time is optimum for realizing the intended goals.

Figure 2.1 - Predevelopment Schedule

A Gantt chart gives everyone an easy-to-understand view of the timelines and expected milestones. It helps visualize when different parts of the project have become the focus, and when expenses are due.

Key Assumptions

This model will work for a 10-unit apartment right up to 300-unit buildings and beyond. If contemplating building phased projects (e.g., three buildings of 100 units for 300 units in total) the model will not work as well since phased building complicates the development. For phased projects, we use a different, more complex, model.

For this model's purposes, the apartment and model will be built from scratch. It will be comprised of a 270-unit structure with 220,000 square feet of net rentable space. The building, in total, is larger than that. However, the model focuses on the part of the building that will realize an income.

We've assumed a mix of 55 percent one-bedroom units of 720 square feet and 45 percent two-bedroom units of 935 square feet. These are fairly large apartment units because the building is located in a suburban community. In a downtown location, unit sizes will be different. And remember, those percentages and sizes are not randomly chosen—they're determined by the market research for that particular area. Beyond the rentable space are the common areas, hallways, a lobby, and various amenities. These add about 15 percent to the building's square footage. We've assumed the building to be of precast construction, comprising of 10 to 15 stories.

The Variables

The base case model comprises many variables, and each have an effect on the financial picture of the development. However, for this book's purpose, we will concentrate on the five most important variables and their impact on the pro forma and the viability of the project as a whole.

Each key variable is split into three parts to bring into focus not only what we think might happen, but also, what could be the best case and worse case scenarios.

Key Assumptions

SENSITIZED ASSUMPTIONS		OTHER ASSUMPTIONS	
Capitalization Rate	**4.00%**	Annual Revenue Inflation	2.0%
Base Case	4.00%	Annual Cost Inflation	2.0%
Best Case	3.75%	Selling Costs	1.0%
Worst Case	4.25%	Min. NOI Coverage	1.1
		Max. LTV @ Stabilization	75%
Construction Loan Interest Rate	**4.00%**	Permanent Loan Interest Rate	3.0%
Base Case	4.00%	Loan Term (years)	25
Best Case	3.75%	Construction Loan Ratio	76%
Worst Case	4.25%		
Construction Period (months)	**30**		
Base Case	30		
Best Case	27		
Worst Case	33		
Lease-up Period (months)	**18**		
Base Case	18		
Best Case	15		
Worst Case	21		
Operating Expense Variance	**0.0%**		
Base Case	0.0%		
Best Case	-5.0%		
Worst Case	5.0%		

Figure 2.2 - Case Key Assumptions

The Investor's Page

The combined development and operating cash flow with a focus on investors' equity net cash flow and associated IRR is called the Investor's Page.

YEAR	1 2020	2 2021	3 2022	4 2023	5 2024	6 2025	7 2026	8 2027	9 2028	10 2029
Stabilized Holding Month	0	0	0	0	0	7	12	12	12	12
Revenue	–	–	–	–	–	4,729,202	8,269,348	8,434,735	8,603,429	8,775,498
Vacancy Provision	–	–	–	–	–	(118,230)	(206,734)	(210,868)	(215,086)	(219,387)
Operating Expenses	–	–	–	–	–	(1,203,317)	(2,104,086)	(2,146,168)	(2,189,091)	(2,232,873)
Stabilized NOI	–	–	–	–	–	3,407,655	5,958,528	6,077,698	6,199,252	6,323,237
Development Cash Flow	(20,723,426)	(12,020,744)	(32,979,563)	(33,890,412)	(13,134,415)	626,671	–	–	–	–
Construction Loan Draw	0	4,744,170	32,979,563	33,890,412	13,134,415	(84,748,561)	–	–	–	–
Construction Loan Balance	0	4,744,170	37,723,733	71,614,145	84,748,561	–	–	–	–	–
Permanent Loan Balance	–	–	–	–	–	92,474,789	91,012,494	88,445,452	85,800,330	83,074,755
Stabilized NOI	–	–	–	–	–	3,407,655	5,958,528	6,077,698	6,199,252	6,323,237
Interest Payment	–	–	–	–	–	(1,607,378)	(2,695,269)	(2,617,190)	(2,536,736)	(2,453,835)
Principal Payment	–	–	–	–	–	(1,462,303)	(2,567,042)	(2,645,122)	(2,725,575)	(2,803,476)
Income Before Tax	–	–	–	–	–	337,973	696,216	815,387	936,941	1,060,926
Valuation @4.00% Cap Rate	–	–	–	–	–	146,042,346	148,963,193	151,942,456	154,981,306	158,080,932
Less: Selling Cost @ 1.00%	–	–	–	–	–	(1,460,423)	(1,489,632)	(1,519,425)	(1,549,813)	(1,580,809)
Less: Loan Balance	–	–	–	–	–	(92,474,789)	(91,012,494)	(88,445,452)	(85,800,330)	(83,074,755)
Net Proceeds From Sale	–	–	–	–	–	52,107,125	56,461,067	61,997,580	67,631,162	73,425,368
IRR Calculation *Based on valuation @ 4.00% Cap Rate*										
Equity Investment	(20,723,426)	(7,276,574)	–	–	–	–	–	–	–	–
Income Before Tax	–	–	–	–	–	337,973	696,216	815,387	936,941	1,060,926
7-Year Cash Flow — IRR 16.5%	(20,723,426)	(7,276,574)	–	–	–	8,352,908	57,157,283	815,387	–	–
10-Year Cash Flow — IRR 14.7%	(20,723,426)	(7,276,574)	–	–	–	8,690,881	696,216	815,387	936,941	74,486,294

Figure 2.3 - Cash Flow - Investor's Page

The Executive Summary

The key thing to understand is that a 25-point spread in cap rates results in the value of the building going up or down by 8 to 10 million dollars.

SCHEDULE

	FROM	TO	MONTHS
Land Purchase	Jan-20	Jan-20	0
Predevelopment	Feb-20	Aug-21	18
Construction Period	Sep-21	Mar-24	30
Lease-up	Oct-23	Apr-25	18
Stabilized	May-25	May-25	0

OVERVIEW

Net Operating Income @ Stabilization	5,841,694	5,841,694	5,841,694
Capitalization Rate	4.25%	4.00%	3.75%
Valuation @ $3.06 per SQFT AVG revenue	137,451,619	146,042,346	155,778,502
Selling Costs @ 100%	(1,374,516)	(1,460,423)	(1,557,785)
Sales Proceeds	136,077,103	144,581,922	154,220,717
Total Costs	(112,121,890)	(112,121,890)	(112,121,890)
Profit Before Taxes if Sold	**25,955,213**	**32,460,032**	**42,098,827**
Return on Cost	**21.4%**	**29.0%**	**37.5%**
IRR Upon Stabilization if Sold		16.8%	
IRR 10-Year		14.7%	

UNIT MIX

UNIT TYPE	SQFT	No. UNITS	% OF TOTAL	RENT	$/SQFT
Total Res Units	220,630	270	100%	2,076	2.54
Average Res	817			2,076	2.54

DEVELOPMENT COSTS

	TOTAL	PER RES UNIT	PER SQFT	%
Land	15,450,000	57,222	70	13.8%
Construction	72,000,000	381,111	326	64.2%
Professional Fees	3,426,500	12,691	16	3.1%
Development Management	3,300,000	12,222	15	2.9%
Permits and Approvals	5,266,800	19,507	24	4.7%
Marketing and Leasing	1,835,736	6,799	8	1.6%
Financing and Interest	10,608,321	60,829	74	9.5%
Taxes, HST, VAT	5,815,439	21,539	26	5.2%
Operating Income During Lease-up Incl. Sec Deposit	(5,580,905)	(20,670)	(25)	-5.0%
Total Development Costs	112,121,890	415,266	508	100%

CONSTRUCTION FINANCING

Construction Loan	84,788,270	76%	
Equity	27,333,620	24%	(Total slightly diff from DCF)
Total	112,121,890	100%	

Figure 2.4 - Executive Summary

As you can see, the return-on-cost can vary from 21 to 37 percent. Cap rate makes a huge difference to the return. A developer should be trying various scenarios during the sensitivity analysis to determine what their profit might be. Remember, cap rate is determined not by the developer—or us—but by the marketplace and the buyer at the time. Having multiple offers is typically going to drive the cap rate down.

The Base Case Summary

These are the headline numbers for the base case. It's a summary of achieved financial results, with references to the base case numbers.

SENSITIZED ASSUMPTIONS		HEADLINE NUMBERS	
Capitalization Rate	**4.00%**	NOI at Stabilization	5,841,694
Base Case	4.00%	Capitalization Rate	4.00%
Best Case	3.75%	Valuation @ $3.06 per	146,042,346
Worst Case	4.25%	sqft Avg Revenue	
		Less: Selling Costs	(1,460,423)
Construction Loan Interest Rate	**4.00%**	Sales Proceeds	144,581,922
Base Case	4.00%	Total Cost	(112,121,890)
Best Case	3.75%	Profit Before Taxes if	
Worst Case	4.25%	Sold at Stabilization	32,460,032
		SPREAD=120 bps	
Construction Period (months)	**30**	Return on Cost	29.0%
Base Case	30	Development Yield	5.2%
Best Case	27		
Worst Case	33	IRR Upon Stabilization if Sold	16.8%
		IRR 10-year	14.7%
Lease-up Period (months)	**18**		
Base Case	18	Construction Cost Per Unit	415,266
Best Case	15	Construction Cost Per SQFT	508
Worst Case	z21	Value Per Unit at Stabilization	540,898
		Value Per sqft at Stabilization	662
Operating Expense Variance	**0.0%**		
Base Case	0.0%		
Best Case	-5.0%		
Worst Case	5.0%		

Figure 2.5 - Base Case Headline Numbers

Notice that the average total revenue of $3.06 per square foot is time adjusted, and that the spread between the development yield and the per-month cap rate is 120 basis points. As the cap rate increases, this spread reduces—and vice versa.

Also take note of the sale value per square foot of $662 against the cost of $508. The 10-year IRR will generally be less than the short period IRR if the project is sold earlier. We've calculated a profit of $32 million for this base case project.

Stressing the Proposed Business Model

The purpose of stress testing the financial model is to determine the effects of changing costs, whether they move up or down. We can now play with multiple "what if?" scenarios, using the base case, best case, and worst case as starting points. By changing one or more values, we can adjust the model to determine what effects we might experience on the project's financials.

Once a model is built, it's up to the analyst in charge to "play" around with the model to determine a project's viability against unanticipated or selected changes. This can include changes to the development schedule, construction delays, cost overruns, or a reduction in achievable rents—a developer must be prepared for any eventuality. Although with rigorous rent-setting procedures and appropriate market knowledge, it's unlikely that rents will be overestimated. However, it's still important to be prepared for the worst in order to succeed in the face of any unexpected situation.

Raising the Rents

First, let's examine some positive scenarios:

- What changes to the development's profit does a 5 percent increase in rents make?
- What happens if the operating costs are reduced by 5 percent?
- What if hard costs are reduced by 5 percent?

Having a functional model gives us valuable insights into the effects of those scenarios on profitability. Now, the example assumes an arbitrary 5 percent change to a few variables. However, there are many other variables to consider, such as lease-up time (longer and shorter), construction time frame, budget overruns, etc. The model can easily predict the effects to the changes of those variables as well.

The table below (Figure 2.6) displays the difference in overall valuation that can be experienced by either increasing rent by 5 percent or reducing operating expenses or construction costs by 5 percent.

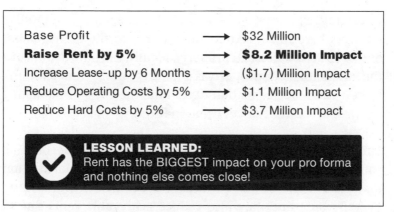

Base Profit	⟶	$32 Million
Raise Rent by 5%	⟶	**$8.2 Million Impact**
Increase Lease-up by 6 Months	⟶	($1.7) Million Impact
Reduce Operating Costs by 5%	⟶	$1.1 Million Impact
Reduce Hard Costs by 5%	⟶	$3.7 Million Impact

LESSON LEARNED:
Rent has the BIGGEST impact on your pro forma and nothing else comes close!

Figure 2.6 - Impact Analysis Results

This table highlights how rent changes have the greatest impact on the development model's results and the property's overall valuation. Therefore, designing a building to collect the highest rents should be the developer's primary focus. Raising rents by 5 percent increases profit by \$8.2 million. If operating costs are reduced by 5 percent—which is a lot more difficult to do—profits rise by about \$1.7 million. Reducing your hard costs by 5 percent increases profits by \$3.7 million, but this too is difficult and may require a reduction in material quality and a lower level of refinement.

The Ultimate Purpose

The purpose of this exercise is to determine what elements of the entire project have the greatest effect on profitability.

Ultimately, rent has the most impact on a property's overall valuation. Not only does it make the biggest difference, but it also remains the most likely variable to be altered. This is because rents are based on what the market can sustain, the availability of a unit type, features, finishes, and lastly, the level of skill the project's leasing agent can apply to achieving the highest rents possible.

Operating expenses have a lower impact on profitability. Changes here mean significant changes to the management and overall function of a property. Ideally, the time to improve the functioning of a property is during the design and planning stages, when decisions that determine the costs of managing the property have not yet been finalized.

Similarly, reducing construction costs involves renegotiating contractor agreements or using lower-quality construction materials. This can have a drastic outcome on a property's overall value and may also reduce achievable rents due to cheaper finishes. In the end, the property may no longer be competitive.

An extended leasing process may increase your carrying costs, but it can also enable the property to achieve higher rents, which will increase the overall NOI and subsequently improve profitability. The model assumes a loan of about $84 million at 4 percent interest. If lease-up were extended by six months, the cost of leasing would increase by approximately $1.6 million. However, this expense is nowhere near the $8 million increase in value which could have been achieved by further pushing rents during this extended period.

Time is not necessarily the most important variable during lease-up. Of course, the developer will do everything they can to lease a building as fast as they can—that only makes sense. But driving the rent up as high as they can has a long-lasting, significant impact.

Operating Costs

Some advocate spending as much time as possible in order to reduce operating costs. In concept, reducing those costs is a good thing. However, the execution of getting there is not quite so cut and dried. If operating costs have been reduced by 5 percent because everything has been perfectly set up (lights on timers, water-flow controlled, etc.), profit only rises by about $1 million. Yet, by focusing on getting the best possible rent, profits go up by $8 million.

Hard Costs

A 5 percent reduction of hard costs results in $3.7 million extra profit. But getting those costs down that far is a Herculean task.

Ideally, the rents should be up 5 percent, and operating and hard costs down 5 percent. But the effort to get those percentages is not shared equally. Do what gets the best increase in profits with the least effort.

Our Model Can Be Yours

If you're interested in this model and want a demonstration of what it can achieve for your projects, we'd be happy to discuss it in detail.

Refer to our FULL Service Experience™
in Figure 0.5 on Pg xxvii

Normally, we closely guide a client through the complete process. That process normally occurs after we do our initial feasibility study. The feasibility study provides the inputs for the client's rent, unit type and unit mix, and operating costs. Once construction costs are added, we build this model to their needs and stress test it.

Conclusion

The base case scenario resulted in a return of 32 percent—a very good pro forma!

By raising rents by 5 percent, profits rise by $8 million. Compare that to taking six months longer to lease the building, which only impacts profit by $1.7 million. Leasing can be as fast as possible so long as there's no sacrificing the rental rate. The two aren't proportionally tied together—both can be done at the same time. By reducing operating costs, we gain $1.1 million, and by reducing hard costs, we gain $3.7 million. The biggest impact by far is rent—nothing else comes close.

The lesson: when designing a building, design
it to get the highest rents possible.

Through the lease-up service that we provide, we can convert the uncontrollability of rent into a controllable element. That is essentially what we bring to the client's table.

Montreal — La MARQ 515: A Sales Story

Challenge

La MARQ 515 is a landmark luxury student housing apartment building that once was an office building. However, getting it built was challenging.

Although building student housing typically results in higher profit margins than conventional apartments, there are nuances and challenges that developers must understand. One of those is that student housing is by far the most location sensitive business in all of real estate. The land must be in close proximity to a university in order for the building to be viable.

Montreal, Quebec, has the largest student population in the country. McGill University, centrally located, is one of Canada's best universities. But finding a site to build student housing in that area is nearly impossible. What was possible, was buying a 10-story office building with the intention to convert it into student housing.

However, conversions are far more challenging than conventional apartment developments. The developer must build in larger contingencies to cover unexpected issues. There also must be a greater reward to compensate for the added risks that come from the extra time, materials, and costs, and unanticipated obstacles that more conventional developments don't encounter.

Action

My client, Auburn Developments, a family-run company, hired me to identify the best place to build student housing in Canada. I came back to them with a business plan that went beyond one project—there was a programmatic opportunity available: build luxury student housing across the country.

The family invited me to participate in the deal. My job was to find land, the architect, and put the deal together. The existing building was then gutted, and an 11th floor added. During construction, there were major challenges with the existing floor plate and bracing. Those challenges pushed back the building's opening for one year.

I became intimately involved in the design of the building, its construction, conversion issues, architects, city planners, construction engineers, and finally, students, during lease-up and move-in. I actually lived in the building for lease-up, meeting with parents and students from all over the world.

In the end, we had converted a 10-story office tower into a 100-apartment, 440-bed, luxury student housing building.

Result

La MARQ 515 was a revolutionary project; the first A-Class luxury building for student housing, and a benchmark project for me because of my continued involvement in the project. I quickly became well versed in zoning application and building design while working with architects, contractors, and planning officials.

What we had achieved was to take an already proven US student housing model and replicate it in Canada for the first time. We proved that the amenity-rich model does work in Canada. Subsequently, many other luxury student housing buildings were built on this model.

It's rare for a broker to get involved in the development of a building. This way of doing things became a precursor for our current *Apartment Development FULL Service Experience*™ process. This business model—find the site, consult with the developer, work with the development teams, lease and sell— was the genesis behind the full service and coaching we offer developers today. We do everything but take up a hammer and put up the funds. In this case, we were more than a broker; we were the de facto partner.

Testimonial: Karen Crich, Auburn Developments

We retained Derek to search for a student housing site across Canada. In his report back to us, he included a business plan for luxury student housing developments that incorporated business plans and models that were successful not only in Canada, but also in the United States.

Derek identified a site in Montreal, an ideal location based on the student population and student housing available at the time. During the process we relied on Derek for many things, including the acquisition of the site, the layouts and amenities that were incorporated during the development and construction of the building, the lease-up, initial staffing and management of the building, and the ultimate sale of the completed building to a third-party.

In my opinion, Derek is the expert on student housing in Canada.

Street view

Common area games room

Common area lounge

Figure 2.7 - Montreal - La Marq 515

Apartments of the Future

Introduction

The renter of tomorrow may, on the surface, look like the renter of yesterday, but this renter is, in fact, a new breed—a product of uncertain economic, political, environmental, and technological landscapes. These factors influence these renters' housing decisions and how they see themselves living in an ever-changing world. Similarly, today's developers see the opportunities inherent in those changes, designing multifamily housing with lower operating costs, space-saving designs, and yet, still able to attract the modern renter with compelling innovations and outstanding functionality.

The Current Situation

Despite the ongoing need for one-bedroom units in all markets, two-bedroom units remain popular.

PROJECT NAME	HEIGHT (FLOORS)	UNITS	UNIT TYPE ST	1	1+D	2, 2+D	3, 3+D	UNIT SIZE (SQ FT) ST	1	1+D	2, 2+D	3, 3+D
Bay Gerrard	43	595	18.5 %	47.1 %	–	29.1 %	5.3 %	435	629	–	862	1090
Regent Park Block 30	30	346	7.5 %	41.3 %	–	35.6 %	14.7 %	360-517	451-665	–	597-1090	936-1435
666 Spadina	13	113	–	31.8 %	2.7 %	54.9 %	10.6 %	–	527-780	723-742	716-1101	1046-1470
2525 Bathurst	13	149	0.7 %	74.5 %	–	21.4 %	3.4 %	428	483-789	–	780-850	1110-1309
45 Lisgar, Toronto	14	291	1.8 %	20.7 %	21.1 %	47.0 %	9.4 %	420	510	575	780-850	950
King St/Springhurst	36 & 18	913	17.4 %	62.5 %	3.4 %	15.2 %	1.5 %	385	434	–	585	916
939 Eglinton	18	262	–	24.1 %	25.6 %	50.3 %	–	–	525	660	790-850	1065
Eastdale Road and Dufferin	35	484	–	38.2 %	20.5 %	16.6 %	24.7 %	–	523	639	720	1025
5950 Bathurst	16	230	–	23.0 %	22.6 %	44.4 %	10.0 %	–	550	625	775-875	–
475 Patricia, Toronto	10	240	–	27.1 %	31.3 %	41.6 %	–	–	550	625	775-875	–
9251 Yonge St, Richmond Hill	43 & 39	960	–	26.0 %	36.5 %	37.0 %	0.5 %	408	550	580	785-875	950
Block 8 Phase 1	37	428	12.6 %	43.9 %	0.5 %	41.4 %	1.6 %	408	552	600	810	1120
Harwood and Bayly Ajax 2	25	308	–	26.0 %	32.4 %	41.6 %	–	–	447-600	620-656	730-852	–
Adelaide Extension Ottawa	27	228	–	90.4 %	0.5 %	8.7 %	–	–	458-663	–	1006-1244	–
One Tower	37	379	0.9 %	63.6 %	–	36.4 %	–	–	461-488	–	723-884	–

Figure 3.1 - Unit Sizes and Types

The graphic in Figure 3.1 shows the unit mix and sizing, unit count, and density, in projects across the Greater Toronto Area (GTA), Ottawa, and Calgary. Across the board, the bulk of the units are one- and two-bedroom units. Regardless of location, market position, or market preferences, there is always a need for one-bedroom units that cater to the broadest potential resident base.

Purpose-built rental apartments are often larger than comparable condo units in many markets because condos are designed to meet a price point and maximize resident appeal to better compete against local rental properties. The average one-bedroom plus den rental runs around 725 square feet, versus 660 square feet for condos. Two-bedroom units and two-bedroom plus den are in the 750 to 850 square foot range, and some on the list go over 1,000 square feet. These larger sizes, frankly, are not common in condos any longer.

Building for the affordable housing market, often with grants or incentives from different levels of government, will change the unit mix based on the subsidy program. With an aim for more flexibility in the living space, using space-saving devices like the Murphy bed, dens become more useful. Space-saving devices also facilitate working from home, whether it be temporary or, as we're seeing in some cases, a permanent arrangement.

The Changing Rental Landscape

Building for the future is here. It's not some obscure concept that we can put off until tomorrow, building as we have done through the years. It demands we not only react, but also, lead the way through innovation and creative thinking.

The challenges of future apartment design are these:

- Changing renter demographics/the boomer boom
- Finding innovative designs to maximize interior space functionality, including work-from-home spaces
- Utilizing durable and easily cleaned materials
- Repurposing existing structures to regain value
- Incorporating technological advancements and IoT (Internet of Things) devices to minimize operating expenses and promote renter satisfaction
- Maximizing land use to increase profitability

The Boomer Boom

Baby boomers are the fastest growing cohort in our society. They're growing faster than the millennials and tend to have more disposable income. The boomer does not want to rent a condo because tenure is important to them. They want a practical rental where they can live out the rest of their lives without maintenance responsibilities.

With more money to spend, boomers want a larger space that won't look dated in a few years, retaining its like-new appearance. They often desire parking for two cars and amenities that give them the perks they had in their former homes. They also expect spacious kitchens, full-size appliances, in-suite storage (instead of a locker in the basement), and some form of outdoor space, like a balcony that can act as an extension of their living space.

The Post-pandemic Paradigm

The COVID-19 pandemic has brought about some unexpected changes to the apartment development industry. Some of the changes have been reactionary and some have been "sticky."

The sticky changes are the better and smarter ways of doing things. After years of developing a certain way, often without thinking about it (or if they had, thought the difficulty in retooling too challenging), the pandemic has challenged that status quo. It's a true testament to human ability and agility that we can reinvent ourselves as communities to meet those challenges. There are many lessons that the industry has learned about the future of apartment living. Many of those sticky changes will endure and should be carried forward.

An important one is the sharp increase in percentage of individuals working from home. The shift to working at home is here to stay. Though we don't know to what degree, it's probably not going to be 100 percent; but it may be nearly 30. Those working from home have proven they can do it; therefore, we must deliver the right spaces for it. We've all seen individual workspaces due to the sharp increase of online meetings. To be frank, some of those spaces are not very work-friendly. But by designing multifamily products with spaces within the footprint where people can work for hours at a time with natural light and ventilation, developers can provide units that are very attractive to the work-at-home renter.

These design changes do impact unit affordability. The current trend is to smaller units, which are cheaper to build. Added work-at-home space pushes up unit sizes, driving prices higher again. To keep prices low, flexible design and adaptable common spaces allow residents more uses within the building.

Less Space, Improved Livability

Prototypes for Different Densities

A whole new range of multifamily units have been designed based on three principles:

- Delivering the most efficient apartment that can be built for a given prototype
- Achieving the highest density
- Making those products easy and/or affordable to build

The importance of these new prototypes is actually simple, and illustrated by the following graphic, which outlines the basic efficiency metrics of a variety of design prototypes.

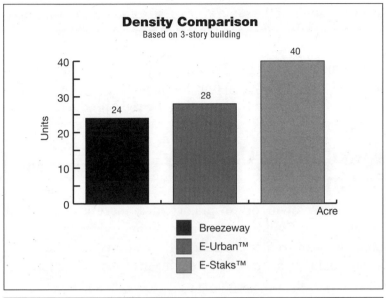

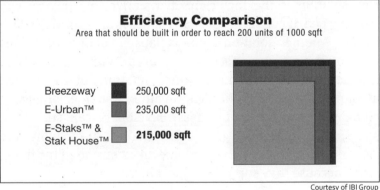

Figure 3.2 - Density Comparison

In the US, the density of a typical, three-story garden apartment—called a Breezeway Building—is about 24 units per acre. However, through the introduction of new design principles, the overall density of a project can be drastically increased; a similar parcel of land being capable of accommodating up to 40 units per acre.

With a more efficient design method, costs can be further reduced as more units can be built on a smaller footprint. The same 200 units of the same average size and the same number of stories might only need five acres instead of eight.

Depending on the region, it could be a saving of $120 to $150 a square foot. With a 200-unit development, a developer can save up to $5 million by delivering the right product.

Maximizing Usability in Small Spaces

In the downtown core of major cities, there is a trend for developers to build smaller apartments, which have been popular with renters. Though these units can be more affordable, they are more challenging in terms of functionality.

One solution is the inclusion of a simple, old device—the Murphy bed. It converts a sleeping space into a working space by day. Another solution is the collapsible sliding partitions that can reconfigure spaces as required. With smart design, it is possible to create highly functional units in a restricted amount of space. With the right furniture and interior design, along with naturally lit spaces, developers can still build small units but deliver great functionality. By including the right mix of amenities, they become an extension of the living space because they support modern lifestyles.

To maximize efficiency and accessibility for residents, in multibuilding projects it is often advantageous to amalgamate amenities into a single floor in one building as opposed to being spread across each building. Rooftop amenities can be positioned on one building while ground floor amenities occupy another for all-season use.

Repurposing Existing Structure

"It's often more beneficial to renovate an existing structure than to begin from scratch."
— Derek Lobo

The times we currently live in have created the right scenario for conversions to occur.

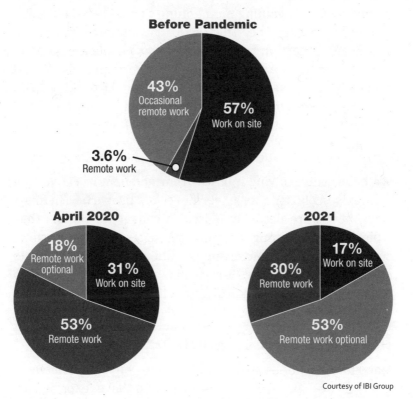

Courtesy of IBI Group

Figure 3.3 - Work-at-home Trends

Can I see a future where part of every week, certainly part of every month, a lot of our employees will be at home? Absolutely.

— James Gorman, Morgan Stanley

All economies move through cycles. A downturn can create the right opportunity for conversion of other asset classes to multifamily buildings, and underperforming assets can be recalibrated to meet market demand.

Housing prices remain stable, or in some cases, are undergoing significant increases regardless of macroeconomic conditions and as demand outstrips supply. Across North America, retail intensification is gaining momentum. The increase in online commerce is dramatic. The rise of e-commerce has had a significant impact on retail space. Fewer people are going to shopping centers, which tend to sit on large parcels of land primarily occupied by an endless sea of surface parking. With the demand for surface parking somewhat diminished, land can be freed up and now used for multifamily residential housing.

We have seen growing interest from hoteliers in converting their existing hospitality assets into rental properties. In many ways, hotels are perfectly poised to convert to rental—they typically have strong amenity packages and understand customer service. Converting traditional hotel rooms into rental appropriate suites is a science, and hoteliers looking to convert should engage a professional team to assist.

Benefits and Challenges

Many municipalities are already open to conversion between asset classes, particularly in areas that have experienced economic downturns with closures across commercial, industrial, or hospitality uses. We believe that there will likely be accommodations by municipalities to allow apartment developers to convert these spaces to a more viable use. With an alignment of ideals and needs, municipalities will facilitate the conversion of existing properties in order to increase the amount of available housing options.

Because the developer is dealing with a conversion site, it means construction generates less waste, has less of an environmental impact, reduces labor time and cost of construction due to existing parking (some below grade), and has a core and shell already in place. Most importantly, conversions keep neighborhoods vibrant, and cities looking refreshed and active. Development in an active community encourages strong local amenities that will drive rents and ultimate value. From the city's perspective, conversions reduce the amount of unoccupied, derelict buildings, and make room for negotiation within the planning process.

Though conversion between asset classes is not completely straightforward—there are challenges—we believe all of these can be overcome with the right development team.

Technology Is Everywhere

Historically, technology has been retrofitted into our existing living spaces. But with the demand for tech increasing, the need for that tech to be integrated into our living spaces is growing quickly.

Transforming the Apartment of the Future

We're all used to smartphones, streaming services, and electric cars, but the technology list grows longer every day. Smart appliances are now in stores. Lighting (and much more) can be controlled by switch, device, or voice. And we're now working from home, expecting our home "office" to be as functional as our traditional office. All this requires fast and reliable broadband, in-suite Wi-Fi, and fast mobile connections.

Apartments are already being designed differently, accommodating bright, dedicated working spaces, and improved connectivity. Surfaces are now expected to be made of durable materials that are easy to keep clean.

Shoppers now make about half their purchases online—that percentage will surely grow. All those packages need to be delivered quickly and safely, necessitating the need for increased locker space, where deliveries can be left without staff intervention, the purchaser notified, and then, retrieved securely. This includes the ability to accept over-sized packages and safe food (with perishables) storage.

The amenity package has been transformed dramatically. We now see demand for features like rock-climbing walls, immersive fitness abilities, and state-of-the-art exercise tech. Developers need to incorporate several smaller private areas for people to work from. The ability to add these larger ticket items will, of course, vary. Larger buildings in major markets will add these, while smaller buildings in secondary and tertiary markets will need to be very creative, with a more limited amenity space offering.

Along with interior changes, the market (particularly subsidized government lending programs) is demanding the building itself be environmentally sustainable. There's a growing trend for constructing carbon-neutral buildings with high-efficiency heating/cooling designed with passive heating and heat island cooling.

Resident parking will be transformed as well. The growing number of electric bikes and scooters need space while electric cars require access to charging stations.

The Digital Twin

The concept of the digital twin is simple: think of the entire building represented digitally. This includes the mechanicals, electrical, heating and cooling system, intercom, and monitoring, and with both management-facing and resident-facing components.

Figure 3.4 - The Digital Twin

Using AI and machine learning, and IoT, property owners and managers can better monitor the systems within a building and ensure that any potential issues (such as a vacant unit's temperature falling too low, water leak, or major mechanical/electrical malfunction) are tracked before they can cause harm.

From reducing energy usage by tracking peak and low usage periods, to adjusting how mechanical systems function, the goal is to monitor usage and better align the mechanical and technical systems of a building with the usage patterns of the residents.

From the resident's point of view, they would be able to view their unit's utility usage, rental payments, any messaging to the building's management (such as malfunctions, outages, requests for service, delivery notifications), and status of any all-building alerts or requests.

From a management perspective, they could monitor (minutely and trend-wise) and alter any of the building's mechanical, electrical, and heating/cooling to keep the building working at peak efficiency. For example, if management found that hot water usage was low at certain times, they could reduce the amount of hot water generated for those times, thus saving on heating costs. By improving a building's efficiency, the life cycle of various components could be extended for the benefit of both renter and owner.

For both residents and management, an ongoing dialogue of building-related matters keeps everyone in the loop, thus eliminating surprises on both sides, and fostering a community-friendly atmosphere.

Placemaking

"It's difficult to design a space that will not attract people. What is remarkable is how often this has been accomplished."

– William Whyte

A Sense of Place

A well-informed design, which takes into account the needs of residents and the community, can elevate an apartment from a mere space to a place. A sense of place is a term that reflects our emotional reaction and perception when we visit a certain place. It's our relationship with that place in our bodies, our experiences and activities, our memories of the past, and that place's unique identity.

Place is to space as person is to body. Places have identities, spaces have objects. Places have histories and meanings to the users, which go beyond the physical elements. We need to remember that the space between buildings is just as important as the buildings themselves. This is the place that people gather and connect. Designing with those spaces in mind can foster a deeper sense of place and belonging for the people, and for the community as a whole.

Why Is It Important?

There are many interpretations of what placemaking is, what it means, and its purpose. In addition, placemaking is a very hot subject both for real estate professionals and urban planners and architects.

It's often said: "You know it when you see it."

A great space has something to do with the number of people engaged in a place that has a certain charm, if not beauty. It's a space that's easy to get to, and where people feel safe and connected to the location and community. Place is that something extra, that vibe that a person gets when they first walk into a place that seems to draw them in.

Creating a development that is a place rather than a space will drive rents by making the community more desirable to live in for future residents.

How Do We Get from Space to Place?

Placemaking is not necessarily a single thing or something easy to define, and it's not a single tool. It's a set of best practices. It's an ongoing set of processes and activities that develop, define, and maintain a space.

The look of the building matters, but we also must grasp how that building can become a place of meaning; how it can become a home. In the multifamily industry, we know that each renter wants to get the most out of their money, and it's not just about luxurious amenities or high-end finishes.

Placemaking is making a physical space that empowers people to create spiritual, emotional, and psychological connections. What we like to hear and what we often see is that placemaking is a process of creating quality places where people want to live, work, play, shop, learn, and visit.

The creation of quality spaces is a means to an end. Walkable, friendly places generate vibrancy. They build a sense of community that leads to creativity, wellness, and collaboration. These are all elements we believe are vital to a successful community development. If places are attractive and vibrant, they often yield higher commercial and economic benefits for businesses, developers, and owners.

A developer can incorporate elements of placemaking through strong signage that matches the company brand, creating walkable spaces exterior to their building, and creating communal gathering spaces.

Conclusion

Innovative design, which is responsible design, is the way of the future. Adopted appropriately, such design has significant potential to drive rents. But that doesn't mean just integrating new technologies and materials, or even novel ways of using interior and exterior space. It means listening even more closely to the needs of the renters and designing buildings for them. Understanding the target renter will guide the developer to the appropriate technologies and design concepts in order to maximize their experience, and in turn, drive their rents.

Target residents are the ones who will provide the impetus to innovate and bring improved designs to the marketplace. By designing a building that's more attractive than the competition's, it will command a premium.

Looking down the road of the future is not easy. Apartment buildings last many years. Designing them to maintain their attractiveness as they age is challenging. Technology changes quickly, new trends overwhelm older ones in the blink of an eye. Outside forces, such as the COVID-19 pandemic, change markets indelibly. Adapting to demographic changes is easier, but only because of their relatively predictable nature. The only constant is change.

By keeping our ears to the ground, and constantly updating our knowledge of renter expectations, market and demographic trends, technological advances, and lifestyle expectations, we can meet the future's challenges successfully and compellingly.

✓ Ottawa—Terrasses Gabrielle Apartments: A Sales Story

Challenge

Second-generation developers, Francis Lépine and Francesca Lépine-Willson, had a vision to build a large apartment business. With their family's firm, they had already built 25 buildings. However, they wanted to go out on their own and prove that this concept of building purpose-built luxury apartments in the capital region was a viable one.

Action

When there is a grand vision to build a repeatable model of the apartment of the future, start with one building as a model. Lépine's model building was 411 North River Road, built in a country-casual luxury style. This 117-unit building featured an indoor pool—unusual for such a small apartment building. After completion, successfully leasing up, we sold the building.

The success of this project and the confirmation that their vision of the future was viable, gave Lépine the confidence to go ahead with the Kanata Lakes project.

Result

Lépine then embarked on the Kanata Lakes project. Knowing it was very difficult for a potential buyer to have a clear picture of his vision during the first building's construction phase, we took the buyer for a tour of 411 North River Road so they could see what a prototype, or a smaller version of the Kanata Lakes project, would eventually look like. The buyers were very impressed.

After several years of construction, The William's Court at Kanata Lakes development became, at the time, the largest new apartment transaction in Canadian history, and the largest purpose-built multifamily housing development to be built in 40 years.

Testimonial:
Francesca Lépine-Willson

Our family has built and sold a number of apartments in Ottawa, and Derek's expertise has been a key component. Ours is a long-term and mutually trusting relationship.

Main lobby and entrance

Street view

Indoor swimming pool

Figure 3.5 - Ottawa - Terrasses Gabrielle Apartments

Reducing Municipal Taxes and Operating Costs

Introduction

Although highly successful, once completed and stabilized, purpose-built rental buildings have to achieve long-term stability and be subject to continuous maintenance. Keeping the operations consistent involves a full understanding of the operating costs, the largest components being municipal taxes and utilities.

OPERATING EXPENSE	PER UNIT	60%+ %	BUILDING $
Property Taxes	3,200	46%	864,000
Utilities	1,200	17%	324,000
Management Fee	853	12%	230,379
Staff (Ops & Maintenance)	800	11%	216,000
Repair & Maintenance	700	10%	189,000
Insurance	200	3%	54,000
Marketing	100	1%	27,000
Sub-metering Revenue Share	(96)	-1%	(25,920)
TOTAL EXPENSES	**6,957**	**100%**	**1,878,459**

Figure 4.1 - Annual Operating Expenses

Within any operating pro forma there are many line items, which can potentially reduce operating expenses and improve NOI. In this chapter, we introduce the reader to ways to reduce the impact of two of the key variables.

Focus on the Important Stuff

There's a lot going on throughout the course of constructing an apartment building. Many of these concerns quickly become distractions, taking valuable time and focus away from the items that matter most. Although many of those distractions are important items to consider as they reflect the property's market position and overall design aesthetic, they have limited effect on the property's overall value—which should remain the developer's primary focus.

To keep operating expenses as low as possible, focus on two things—property taxes and sub-metering utilities. These drive profitability.

Municipal Taxes

Accounting for over 45 percent of a building's operating expenses, property taxes are the most significant drag on the pro forma. How much they actually affect a specific building varies on a case-by-case basis, depending on the municipality the property is located in, that municipality's property tax classes, and various provincial regulations.

Some municipalities often desire, and encourage, more new rental construction, offering new developments a special property tax rate that can significantly reduce this expense. However, there is often a need to negotiate for the lowest rate. Negotiating with a city government and its planning department is both an art and a science, best left to professionals. A developer should hire a tax lawyer to speak on their behalf.

The Impact of Property Assessment and Taxation

Our focus is on new construction in Ontario. However, the concepts apply across Canada because the effect of property taxes is equally important everywhere.

Provincial Assessment Impact

Because a property's taxes are determined directly on an assessed value, the cycle of assessments needs to be considered and carefully followed.

The Municipal Property Assessment Corporation (MPAC) in the province of Ontario studies, monitors, and reports property values. It is mandated to update those values every four years with a current date of January 1, 2016. In other words, the assessor looks at the property and determines what it would be worth to a willing buyer or willing seller as of January 1, 2016. That value is then phased in for taxation years of 2017 through to 2020.

Current MPAC information is available on its website at mpac.ca.

The Role of the Tax Negotiator

In addition to the pre-roll negotiations, the appeal tracking mechanisms that are put in place, tax bill management, and the tax budgeting and forecasting that we do, we offer tenant inquiries and dispute resolution.

- Pre-roll Negotiations
- Assessments and Appeal Tracking
- Tax Bill Administration
- Tax Budgets
- Tenant Inquiries and Disputes
- Tenant Tax Recovery Schedules
- Tax Rebate Applications/Appeals
- Tax Refund Tracking
- Collections of Assessment Data and Assessment Authority Information Requests
- Due Diligence

Figure 4.2 - Municipal Tax Services

Due diligence is critical. Whether in the pre-development stages of a new building or potentially acquiring an existing building, due diligence is an integral step taken to ensure fact-based decision-making.

Due Diligence

When a client approaches us with the intention of purchasing a property, one of the most important steps is a full review of the associated tax liabilities. Are there outstanding appeals that are pending? What is the status of those tax applications? Where are they in the assessment cycle? If it's a tenanted property with leases in place, is the plan to demolish that building to allow for redevelopment to a higher and better use at a later date? Are there demolition clauses or other avenues that the new purchaser can deal with in terms of setting out a process in order to ensure a smooth transition to the new development?

Due diligence is a critical and important component and is carried out for all clients who need it.

Demolition, Severance, and Zoning Changes

The impact of the assessed value and the tax class that's applied to that property today can have a significant impact on the planning and the various stages of development. When going through a zoning process, we have to assess current zoning and model the tax classifications to measure the impact on the taxes that may be due after zoning changes.

Highest and Best Use

How can that highest and best use valuation have an impact on the planning and rezoning status of the property? That's probably the most important question we get asked, and one we work through with clients during a project's pre-development period.

Equity, as a tool in the province of Ontario, has a significant impact on the evaluation of similar properties. In other words, if a developer owns five buildings or five properties in a row, and they're all similarly zoned—similar in size, etc.—how does equity play a role?

The answer lies with the assessor. If they apply a consistent value to three or four buildings but the remaining two are higher, we can take advantage of that equity provision and try to draw down the higher values to reduce the tax liability incurred through that time frame. In some situations, equity becomes a very important tool.

Why Use Pre-roll Negotiations?

After the planning stage and tax class conversion, with development land rates in place and a new building coming out of the ground, we have another tool at our disposal. Under the Assessment Act of Ontario, MPAC is allowed to go back two years plus the current year after a building is completed to look at previous assessments and revise its assessed value. This, in turn, can change the tax liability.

- S.33(7) of the Assessment Act allows MPAC to go back two years plus the current tax year and value structures that have been "omitted" from the assessment roll
- This creates various issues for property owners:
  - A potentially large omitted assessment and corresponding tax liability
  - Budgeting and cash flow issues for the owner for the year issued and future years while subject of appeal
  - The need to appeal and adjudicate or try to negotiate a reasonable phase-in of the value
  - The increased cost of appeal, not to mention the years it would take to run the appeal and resolve any or all of the issues
  - The city effectively becomes a third party to the appeal process

Figure 4.3 - Impact of Assessment Act

To take advantage of this tool, our firm has created a protocol to proactively meet with MPAC and the corresponding municipality to try pre-negotiating those values. As a result, we create not only a more reasonable phase-in of those values once the building is completed, but also, we avoid that large, omitted assessment coming onto the property some two to three years later.

The benefit of this program is that it provides an opportunity to structure a reasonable schedule of omitted assessments and corresponding tax liability, and if there are areas that parties still do not agree with, we still maintain the full right of appeal. The municipality is not necessarily a party to that process until the building becomes assessable. That way, we avoid having those parties at the table throughout the negotiation process.

By going through this process, we create the benefit of an understood line item in the expense and balance sheet in addition to a stabilized expense line item.

Expense Breakdown

The following table is the expense breakdown on a multi-residential building.

EXPENSE	NEW CONSTRUCTION	EXISTING BUILDS
Property Tax	8.00%	15.00%
Insurance	1.00%	1.00%
Admin	5.00%	5.00%
Management	5.00%	5.00%
Utilities	15.00%	15.00%
Repairs	8.00%	13.00%
Expense Rate	**42.00%**	**54.00%**

Figure 4.4 - MPAC Expense Breakdown 2016

The table lists the items that make up MPAC's expense ratio for both new and old buildings.

For new construction, MPAC says that we have a line item of property tax, which represents approximately 8 percent of the effective gross income. On the existing builds—older stock buildings built prior to the year 2000, and in this case, a building completed in the 1960s—15 percent of the gross income is allocated because it carries a higher tax rate. Insurance, administration, management, utilities, and repairs are all consistently applied between both the new and the old. For repairs, there's a bit of a difference between new and old buildings.

There's a difference in the expense rates of new and old buildings. The typical expense rate, depending on the geographic location in the province, ranges between about 38 and 42 percent for new builds and from about 49 to 56 percent for the traditional existing multi-residential buildings. Again, it's expressed as a percentage of gross income.

Market Value

To create a market value model, we use different sized units. We apply a fair market rent that is derived by both looking at equity and time-adjusted rents back to the base-year value. We apply a standard expense line item for vacancy. In this scenario, the overall expense ratio is 42 percent. And depending on the location—this is for the city of Toronto—the going-in cap rate for this base year in most portions of the city is around 3.25 percent. (Note: the cap rate is assigned by MPAC and is not the real value of the buildings. See below.)

The rent roll plays a vital part since the property's value is based on the current achievable rents. The cap rate is used to inflate the cost based on investor demand and potential rental upside. This is the standard valuation method used when determining the value of an existing asset. From that, we can then apply the tax rates to arrive at the estimated current value: assessment times the tax rate equals liability.

Things to Remember

Expense Ratios

We also want to note that municipalities calculate taxes using certain expense ratios. In our opinion, that's not necessarily the best way to do so since those ratios aren't necessarily rooted in reality. They are based on an average value and do not account for the variability between developments, which can either increase or decrease the operating expense ratio relative to those used by the municipality. They're just a fixed method municipalities use, even though they don't apply well to a particular building.

For most newly constructed multi-residential buildings, expenses run at 25 up to 29 percent—whereas MPAC is applying a much higher rate of around 40 to 42 percent.

Cap Rates

One important discussion we've had time and time again relates to the cap rates MPAC applies to new builds. MPAC currently uses lower cap rates than the market can truly support because they're not based on a property's age. Where it may use a 3.25 percent cap rate, it should actually be 4.5 percent. This value is based on the cap rates achieved by recently transacted new-stock rental buildings as opposed to an average across the spectrum of multi-residential transactions.

Our Advice:
With all the different taxation scenarios,
having dedicated professionals to negotiate
tax rates really makes a difference to a
developer's peace of mind as well as to
their bottom line.

Utilities

In a typical building, utilities account for about 17 percent of the operating expenses. To reduce this expense, sub-metering a building's utilities transfers a sizable portion of this expense to the tenants, decreases total utility consumption, and helps the environment in the process.

While all utility costs can be sub-metered, there's strategy involved if a developer wants to ensure their choices best suit a particular development. Once that strategy is mastered, it's a win-win for both owners and residents. Most new buildings implement some form of sub-metering (heat, electricity, and water), and separating common area utility usage from that of the individual tenants.

Typically, we get involved with developers early in every new project during the initial discussion stage of design and development in order to decide what utilities can be sub-metered and what makes sense for their particular market.

There are many sub-metering companies that can facilitate the process, provide the data needed to make an informed decision, and often, offer rebates for the use of the equipment via installation credits or monthly revenue sharing. Such rebates have the added benefit of both reducing the property's monthly utility bills and creating an additional revenue stream—boosting a building's overall NOI and ultimate valuation.

Sub-metering Overview

The most positive aspect of sub-metering is that it eliminates a volatile variable—often a difficult in-suite utility cost to control.

- Eliminates volatile, variable, and difficult-to-control in-suite costs
- Reduces exposure to utility rate increases
- Advances a sustainability agenda
- Lowers GHG emissions
- Increases property value
- Provides transparent, real-time data for buildings and tenants' utilities

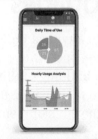

Courtesy of Wyse Meter Solutions

Figure 4.5 - Sub-metering Benefits

If a building's suites are not sub-metered for electricity, water, or thermal, the property owner is paying for those utility costs directly. This leaves the resident with no financial incentive whatsoever to control their usage. While we've seen a steady increase in electricity rates up until last year (about 6 to 8 percent per year), once sub-metered, this is a burden that owners no longer have to bear.

Sub-metering also advances the environment sustainability agenda, which more and more residents are becoming sensitive to. Knowing they're moving into a new building with energy management systems in place gives them assurance that they'll have a positive impact on their carbon footprint.

The biggest financial impact is a significant increase in property value generated from sub-metering. A building will incur reduced expenses, which increases the property's net operating income and drives value into the property.

Added Benefits for Residents

For the residents, sub-metering is also a matter of fairness. What we see on a regular basis is about 10 percent of the residents in a given building use about 25 percent of the power and water.

- Eminently fair. With 10% of residents using 25% of the total energy, residents stop subsidizing their neighbor's utility waste
- Aligns with evolving attitudes and lifestyle choices
- Online tools make it simple to monitor usage and make lifestyle changes
- Motivates residents to conserve and only pay for what they use in-suite

Courtesy of Wyse Meter Solutions

Figure 4.6 - Sub-metering Benefits for Residents

In effect, this means that the majority of residents are subsidizing the highest users—and those users are getting a free ride. Most residents make it quite clear, once they understand the implications, that they don't want to subsidize the excessive users. Firstly, they resent the necessary increase in their monthly rent. Secondly, they resent that those users are wasting valuable resources and damaging the environment while doing so.

There are online tracking tools available to renters so they can easily manage their utility usage. These tools consist of text alerts, instant graphs, and information needed to monitor and plan utility usage in a way that lets them modify their behavior and reduce their bills. Studies have shown that sub-metered electricity usage drops about 35 percent, water consumption by about 22 percent, with heating and cooling costs decreasing as well.

The savings to a building owner are dramatic. We don't think there's any other energy management, or energy management technology, that could be implemented in a building that can generate greater savings. And most of these changes are really just behavioral changes from the residents themselves—balancing lifestyle choices with utility usage.

The Bottom Line

From a leasing perspective, renters often prefer sub-metered buildings because this gives them control over their monthly utility costs. From an owner or landlord perspective, sub-metering encourages resident responsibility—residents are much less likely to be blasting their A/C in the summer or overheating in the winter simply because they are responsible for their own bills.

Technology Trends

Electricity and heating/cooling metering, and water-metering technology have changed significantly over time. Other than a huge reduction in physical meter size and communication modules moved to utility areas, the biggest change has been in the way the meter communicates its usage to the utility company through wireless communication technology.

The meter is installed conventionally within each unit (usually hidden in a wall cavity), and then, consumption is wirelessly transmitted to a central collector in the building—no hard wiring required. As a bonus, the meter's sensors provide leak detection and low unit temperature and freeze detection alerts so immediate action can be taken if there are problems.

In-suite water metering picks up about 90 percent of the water used in a building, not only becoming an important utility to measure, but also, one that's billed to the resident, not the building's owner.

Electric Vehicle Charging Stations

Electric vehicle charging is becoming increasingly important in every new construction project. However, regulations differ greatly across Canada. Some locations mandate that 100 percent of parking spaces offer electric charging, while others may only require 20 percent of the parking spaces to offer chargers.

It's a fast-changing marketplace, with new technology hitting the market nearly every day. Building owners can now bill the residents directly for their energy usage when using a designated electric vehicle charger in their parking space. The developer can also have visitor-parking chargers that are billed by the hour. This solution allows visitors to charge their electric vehicle and pay for what they use as if they were at their own home.

Again, the developer needs to make sure they understand the many different regulations in the various municipalities, states, or provinces, across the country.

Billing and Training

The key component of a successful program is making sure that potential residents—when they come in for lease information—have access to an educational package that's easy to understand. They'll want to know what they're responsible for paying, what their costs will be, how to successfully enroll, and the benefits. Because developers often work with third-party sub-metering companies, how they work with, and respect, residents and their usage data becomes very important.

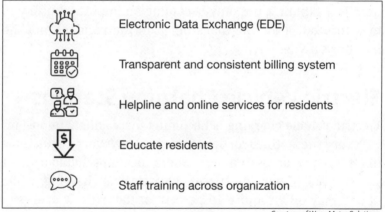

Courtesy of Wyse Meter Solutions

Figure 4.7 - Sub-metering Data Privacy

Sub-metering companies should be using an electronic data-exchange protocol where the billing system is synced with the property management software on a nightly basis, extracting the move-in and move-out information of the resident, and applying that resident data directly to the billing system so that each resident is billed exactly for the months that they are residing there, and no days are lost.

From a resident's perspective, having a mobile app, online support, or a 24/7 number to call when in need of assistance is important to ease the transition to this new system.

Conclusion

Though sub-metering has both its detractors and fans, we think most tenants, when presented with the facts, will prefer sub-metered utilities. The building owners have a different challenge. When compared to their local competition, they assume that potential renters will prefer an all-inclusive rent, and if they elect to install utility sub-metering in their building, they will find their units difficult to rent.

It all boils down to education, which is the responsibility of a building's frontline staff. With proper training and the right educational tools, they should not find it difficult to persuade potential renters that sub-metering is a win for all sides.

There will come a day when there are very few building-wide metered utilities left. Sub-metering technology advances are making it increasingly simple to retrofit an existing building, no matter its age. Gone will be the days when the whole apartment complex is lit up, or tenants keep the air conditioning running all day while they're at work.

Sub-metering is, on many levels, the only way forward.

Conclusion

As a developer, it's all about making a higher profit and a higher margin. Focusing on priorities first: rent, cost of capital, and the two big operating expenses (utilities and taxes) makes all the difference.

Taxes, the biggest operating costs line item, requires careful attention to manage. By bringing in professionals who know the ins and outs of provincial and state or municipal taxation rules, and how to approach government departments, developers stand a good chance of lowering their tax rate as much as possible.

There is also no doubt that managing utility costs should be on a developer's priority list. Once sub-metering is in place, residents quickly realize that being in control of their own usage encourages them to pay more attention to it, and that rents don't have to increase to offset changes in utility rates. Overall, utility consumption drops dramatically. It's a win for tenants, owners, and the environment.

✔ Kingston — Foundry Princess: A Sales Story

Challenge

Yukon-born developer Jay Patry, made his first investment running hockey card trading sessions at the age of 14. A natural entrepreneur, he eventually found his way into the development industry and undertook building the largest wooden building in Canadian history. His chosen market was the newly emerging luxury student housing class.

However, midway through construction, the entire building burnt to the ground. The event made the world's newscasts because of the intensity of the blaze and concerns surrounding large wooden structures.

Patry was not deterred. He rebuilt. But he knew the eventual challenge would be to sell a building, which in its first iteration had made the news so spectacularly. The building was rebuilt to the latest safety standards, with all parties ensuring the building was rigorously inspected and certified by Kingston officials. Patry also fulfilled his own vision of providing luxury student housing. The result was Foundry Princess, one of the most luxurious student housing buildings in Canada.

After completion, the building was fully leased.

Like most developers, Patry wanted to keep his money working for him. After lease-up, he chose our firm to list the building. That choice was largely based on a trip we had taken to Dallas, Texas, years earlier, to view student housing developments in that market. When it came time to sell, we were the logical choice.

Action

How does a developer sell a building that was the scene of the most publicized fire in Canadian history? One would think that event would taint the sale. Our solution was to make its history an advantage.

We declared the fire up front. This was a very well-built building because of what had happened. We repositioned the building from one that had burnt to the ground to one that was the safest and best student housing building available.

The lesson learned here is that, if the developer has a problem with a building, declare it up front and provide lots of information so prospective buyers see the past problems as a strength.

Result

In the end, the building was successfully sold.

Testimonial: Jay Patry, Patry Inc. Developments

I don't think we would have got this deal across the finish line, at this price, with any other broker. Selling a 500-bed student housing community in a tertiary market not only requires knowledge of the asset but also of the buyers and their motivation—something Derek excels at.

Derek and I continue to do business today. For me, this is who I call to get the job done right.

Street view

Rooftop patio area

Private swimming pool

Figure 4.8 - Kingston - Foundry Princess

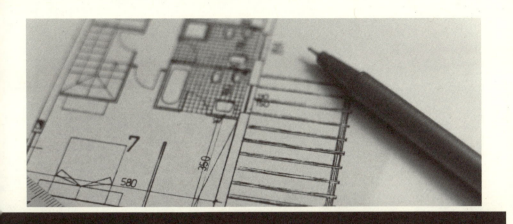

PART 2: Land

Finding and Acquiring Land

Introduction

Apartment buildings sit on land that a developer either acquires without an existing development or when they're intensifying with residential and/or some other asset class occupying the site. So, how does a developer acquire and entitle this land for apartment development?

Land acquisition is a multi-year undertaking. It requires time and research to find suitable land, navigate municipal requirements, assemble a team of professionals, structure a deal, begin due diligence, get the required approvals, close, get permits, have contractors ready, and finally, find financing. Without a good grounding, the process will frustrate many developers. Our aim is to provide the foundations of that process so that our clients come to it with their eyes fully open and prepared for the challenges inherent in the process.

Site Selection

Site selection entails identifying a site or a market to build in, taking on the process of acquiring and entitling the land, and then, continuing with the actual physical development. For this, we conduct an opportunity study.

An opportunities study provides a deep drill into the markets that the developer is interested in building in. We'll complete an economic and demographic analysis to rank the preferred markets, including an analysis of what to build in each market and how much to charge in rent.

There are different indicators a developer should study to make good acquisition decisions. Key among those: population growth, income, the existing rental universe, average rents, and the prevalence of the key renter groups. There are many other indicators, but these are the most important.

Population Growth

As a basic rule of thumb, develop in a community with strong historic and projected population growth. Note that even though many consultants and brokers put an emphasis on major markets, there are many small communities that have seen new, successful developments despite minimal population growth.

In primary markets, an apartment developer is competing head-to-head with condo developers. That's not necessarily the case in small towns—which is an advantage. Smaller municipalities have fewer development applications, and therefore, the approvals process is usually much faster. And since the municipality hasn't typically experienced the high level of interest in development as seen in larger communities, it may be willing to work more closely with interested developers to find a financial solution to help the development process.

The advantages of building in smaller communities are quite real.

The upside in building in smaller centers is that projects can probably make more money and generate more cash flow. But the downside of that is less liquidity and that means a change in the cap rate.

All in all, we're encouraged by the viability of small-town developments for long-term owners. In our opinion, there are very few markets where a developer would not want to develop in.

Age Profile

Every community has its own age profile. Realistically, there are two key age groups that rent: young professionals aged from 20 to 34 and 55+ downsizers.

Younger professionals want a very different rental product than those over 55. They will consider small unit sizes with more limited parking space. The older downsizer is aged from 55 to over 65. They want larger, more luxurious units supported by a different amenity set.

With those two very different products in high demand, developers need to be comfortable building both, and tailoring their product as the community data indicates.

Existing Stock

In a given community, what rental properties currently exist? Basic data from Canada Mortgage and Housing Corporation (CMHC) normally shows all of the rental products in the community. However, new multifamily buildings are competing with apartments that were built from the 60s to the 90s. What's relevant are the rents collected in newer products.

From there, find comparables in existing buildings (both old and new) to understand what rents they're achieving on a unit-by-unit basis. Individual unit comparisons provide more information upon which to decide.

The Rental Pipeline

The land acquisition and the development are multi-year processes. Realistically, even if an opportunity exists today, breaking ground is likely two to three years into the future. Instead of restricting research to what currently exists, find out what's coming down the development pipeline. If upcoming projects are in the pre-construction phase, assume they will be on the market in the next couple of years. If under construction, they may come to market in the next 12 to 18 months.

Knowing what's in the pipeline provides an insight into the competition likely encountered when a particular development comes to market.

Acquiring Land

Land Cost

Land is usually between 10 and 20 percent of the total project cost, with an average of about 15 percent. Therefore, getting the financing and being able to demonstrate to a lender that the market is there in terms of absorption and rental rate is vital. A developer shouldn't go to contract and find out that they can't get a loan because critical information is missing.

Determine what metrics for unit and land costs should be used and what the market valuation looks like for existing transactions before making any offers. Make sure that the proposed land-per-unit is reasonable—don't overpay for land. A lender will not approve land that's too costly.

Existing Conditions

Are there other conditions to that land that affect the valuation? Are there conditions under the soil that have to be dealt with to get the right building foundation? Are there off-site improvements needed, such as a turning lane or running infrastructure to the site, or a municipality-required traffic signal at the location? Those items go dollar-for-dollar off the price of the land.

Onward

Identifying the tract of land that a developer wants to make an offer on is probably the last step. With homework done, a market need established, and achievable rents established that make sense; it's time to begin the process of land acquisition.

Preliminary Due Diligence

Research

One of the more important philosophies when acquiring land is to spend a little money up front to save a lot of money at the back end. Also, research, research, and do more research. There are a lot of data tools and data sources out there to help a developer gather as much data as possible before going to contract. One of the key aspects is to be able to eliminate a site, either for contamination or zoning issues, before getting too far into the process.

- Land use attorney
- Zoning
- Future land use
- Political conditions
- Infrastructure
- Environmental research
- Data

Courtesy of SVN Lotus

Figure 5.1 - Preliminary Due Diligence

Land Use Attorney

The first step in the preliminary due diligence process is to talk to a land use attorney. For this, we advise the services of local attorneys. Outsiders don't have the business relationships nor have their finger on the pulse of the local political environment.

Zoning

What can be done by right? In other words, what does the current zoning classification allow a developer to build so that if/when they finish the submission of their site plan, they have that entitlement by right. It's very difficult to get denied or not get an approval on an entitlement that they have by right.

Future Land Use (FLU)

Many municipalities have what they call FLU maps. This is not the same as zoning. These are plans that the municipality creates that indicate how they see land usage for the future. However, such plans are not a guarantee of the zoning that will be applied to that land.

If a zoning change is required, it usually means public hearings will be needed. Those come with added risk and may take much time to address.

Political Conditions

In addition to local land use attorneys, we recommend hiring civil planners and consultants. Also, talk to other developers who have gone through the process—they may have valuable insights.

> *The importance of using local talent cannot be overstated. They know, and have worked under, the current political conditions. Their knowledge can save a lot of time, headache, and expenses by preventing a developer from proposing something that's not going to get approved.*

Meet with local planning and zoning staff, and any commissions or groups that influence how land is used. Meeting with them very early on in the process may prompt them to provide valuable insights on the changes needed to make a project viable from their point of view.

Infrastructure

The last piece of preliminary due diligence is infrastructure. Is there capacity? Is there adequate access to water and sewer? Are the lines big enough? Sometimes there's access but inadequate capacity. Will the roads need improvements because the project will cause an increase in traffic?

These are all things that aren't readily apparent in a brochure or package. Checking early is vital because it's very difficult to go backwards.

Environmental Research

There are a slew of potential environmental ramifications that might affect a potential site, whether they be above ground or below ground (contamination or buried artifacts of significance). These potentially add a lot of time and additional costs to a project. These have to be identified early, and plans made to deal with them in a timely manner.

Data

Data, data, data, rent comparables, and sales comparables. We live in an information world. The data is out there. If needed, find a consultant who has access to the data needed.

With years of experience, our research team's expertise is second to none in providing this service.

Assembling the Team

Land entitlement and acquisition requires the work of a land use attorney, a civil engineer, and a variety of consultants related to environmental review, traffic, and many more. Remember, use local talent. Find out who has a strong relationship with the municipality, has a track record of getting things approved, as well as being proficient in design.

Land Use Attorney

Before getting into whether or not there are inherent land issues or artifacts on a property, find out if it's even going to be feasible from a by-right or land-use standpoint. A local land use attorney can find out, plus have incentive information and the know-how as to how to deal with zoning issues. And get a read on the mood of the existing planning body.

Civil Engineer

Very early in the process, hire a civil engineer to develop a very basic concept plan—conditions of the site with the zoning and other site development requirements—with an aim to find out if the project is feasible and able to get approval.

Environmental Consultants

After zoning is established and there's a site layout, bring in whatever environmental consultants are needed. In many municipalities, they are required for getting approvals. There may be other permits required in order to address some of the environmental conditions on the site. In some instances, proving to the municipality that there are no environmental contaminants or pitfalls on the property is required. Don't get caught designing a beautiful building only to find out the site cannot be built on.

Site Contractors

The last piece we recommend is finding a site contractor. Once there's a development plan, get an opinion of cost. A civil engineer can help with that—they provide what is called an engineer's opinion of cost. This is especially useful when there are off-site conditions.

Between the civil engineers and the site contractors, a developer will have a good understanding of what costs will be so that they can be built into the pro forma.

Contracts and Comparables

Once a site is settled on and the decision made to make an offer, draw up a contract and begin the comparable sales process. If the site is attractive, how much should it cost? What is the right price to pay for the land? What does the data in the market say about the valuation?

Understanding Comparable Sales

We highly recommend getting all the data possible for comparable sales prior to making any offer, because this will affect the contract.

Timing and Approvals

A milestone schedule helps manage everyone's expectations. Assembly of the team should be completed before beginning this step in order to get a better understanding of what the timeline will be. As a buyer, a developer doesn't want to set an expectation of completing the purchase within a given time frame if there's no possibility of completion within that time.

Usually, the first money spent should be directed to find out if there are issues that will cause the deal to fail. These include environmental concerns, infrastructure inadequacies, and anything else that might render the site not buildable. Once you know that the property doesn't have any issues, start the approvals process. Then, create a set of plans that the buyer knows the municipality will approve.

We can't stress enough the importance of getting timing and approval agreed to up front so that $300,000 into a project the developer doesn't suddenly run out of time, or the market improves to the point where the seller doesn't want to sell.

Subject To Versus As Is

Is your contract a *subject to* or an *as is* contract?

Subject To

A *subject to* contract states: "I have a contingency where I can get my deposit back until I eliminate all unknowns and uncertainties and receive my approvals." This kind of contract eliminates a lot of the buyer's risks. This means the buyer spends money on the professionals mentioned earlier. However, who wants to buy a property and find out they can't build on it?

Many times, sellers won't enjoy that as an offer. A great way to mitigate this kind of situation, from the seller's point of view, is to put a milestone schedule in the contract. This indicates the buyer is spending the money and going through the process. Hopefully, the seller agrees to this and says: "If you're spending money and going through the process, I'm going to continue to give you the time."

As Is

An *as is* contract is usually highly discounted. Roughly half of contracts are *as is*. The risk that a buyer is willing to take cuts the value of that property in half.

Half the value is created by what the buyer does.

Asking the buyer to take this kind of entitlement risk usually cuts the value of a property by 50 percent, and rightfully so, because they do have to spend money to go through that process. Therefore, if they're going to take the risk and spend money without the assurance of the entitlement and the approvals, what the market says is: that developer wants to double his money.

Terms and Conditions

Make sure to dig deep enough into comparable sales to find out if there were any site conditions. A piece of property that sold for $1 million might have otherwise sold for $2 million if it didn't have $1 million in conditions.

Time Value of Money

We definitely structure our contracts so that in a utopian world, the bulldozers show up the day of closing. The internal rate of return, or the time value of the money, starts running the day that property is bought. We recommend structuring the contract as close to the start of construction as possible.

Title and Survey

Make sure there's clear title and a survey and figure out who is paying for those items when completing a contract.

Financing

And finally, in most of the multifamily deals that we see, the construction closing is part of the land closing. Make sure that early in the contract process, there is some idea as to whether or not the lender is in place. A developer doesn't want to go through this expensive process and find out there's no financing available. Take enough time to be sure that in a relatively short period into the contract, financing can be arranged.

Due Diligence

We can now proceed to the actual due diligence. If we have a seller and buyer, and we have a meeting of the minds under contract, what does the process of due diligence look like? How do we make sure there are no unknowns as well as get the approvals needed in order to actually break ground and proceed to construction?

- Preliminary phase
- Environmental assessment
- Zoning
- Budgeting
- Site conditions
- Submittals

Courtesy of SVN Lotus

Figure 5.2 - Due Diligence

Preliminary Phrase

The preliminary phase can be thought of as an insurance policy. Spend a few thousand dollars to find out if there are any environmental issues that may cause liability problems down the road. With a clean preliminary phase (or cleared in later steps), a developer is released of much of the liability if something is discovered later on. We highly recommend this—it may help greatly on the back end.

In addition, we recommend to all clients buying a property to get a survey. Make sure there's no encroachment onto the property—no easements or other conditions that are going to prevent building on the property.

Environmental Assessment

The environmental assessment is to ascertain that there are no artifacts, contaminants, or any other item they may not have thought of that will be a significant cost.

Zoning

Have the right zoning. A land use attorney, civil engineer, and all other professional help should ascertain that a developer has what they think they have or have support they need for what they want to build.

Site Conditions

Soil borings ensure that the ground is suitable for the foundations needed to build upon. Add to this the certainty that the utilities have the capacity to support the project. Go to the utility services and get verification letters.

Take any further steps of assurance that whatever other site conditions found are manageable and are what was discovered during the preliminary due diligence.

Submittals

Now it's time to complete all document submissions. We always recommend enough time to be able to submit. This means get the team together, a design done, then submitted so it can get at least one round of comments from the planning department. That's usually when a developer finds out whether or not they have a site issue. We recommend having enough time built in to get submissions in and gain some feedback.

Approvals

Once through due diligence and there are no obstacles to building left, we come to the approvals process.

Land Use

Land use is what underlies zoning. This is what says that the land is good for residential or multifamily projects.

Zoning

Next is zoning approval. The zoning says that a developer can build residential or multifamily, and its density can be so many units per given area. It's an important piece of information.

We like to tell clients that a deal is highly de-risked once there's zoning approval because the next step is a site plan approval. This is a more detailed level of drawing.

Site Plan

Generally, site plan approvals will not be denied as long as these don't vary from the zoning. It's very difficult for an approval to get denied when the project complies and the developer is not asking for any zoning variances.

Concurrency

Concurrency items are not necessarily managed by the municipality directly. Roads are an example of concurrency. If there's too much anticipated traffic, a developer may face a moratorium on building. Schools are another example—a new residential building may create local school overcrowding.

Once a developer has any needed concurrency letters or approvals, the project is ready for construction.

Construction Permitting

Construction permitting involves the actual plans and specs that a developer is going to build. This is the building department's area. Generally, it's just complying with the building code.

Other Requirements

There may be some other required permits from different government levels or agencies. Ask the land use attorney and civil engineer what approvals will be required for the site. This should be addressed very early in the process.

Closing

With approvals done and a willing seller, we can go on to closing. As for how long this might take, one year is fortunate. Sometimes, it may take up to four years. However, typically, it's between 18 and 36 months from the time a developer goes into a contract until actual construction begins.

Attorney

We always recommend a closing attorney. In North America, title insurance is a big issue—and typically, it is a buyer expense. When negotiating that closing cost, a closing attorney will sometimes not charge for the rest of the closing if they can do the title insurance. This is important. A $15,000 legal bill is not welcome if the developer is also paying the attorney for title insurance.

Equally important, have an attorney review everything to make sure that there is nothing remaining that might derail the deal.

Permits

We highly recommend that buyers structure deals to have the permits in place at closing. We also recommend that contractors are in place and ready to build. It's not necessarily a land function, but don't be caught without a general contractor. Have a full set of plans and specs which, hopefully, includes a building permit. Also, have pricing arranged so that there's no wasted time from closing to when the bulldozers arrive.

Contractors

We always recommend interviewing at least two or three contractors. Whether hiring them for basic site plans or to bid on the construction, it's always better to get more than one opinion.

Financing

Financing is an important part of closing. Usually, we see deals where the land and development closing, or acquisition development and closing loan, is all done at land closing. Ensure that the lender is in place and that there is a development and construction loan in hand when it comes time to close.

Conclusion

The one constant in land acquisition is the length of time it takes to complete—assume it's a long process. And all things being equal, acquisition time is different in different municipalities.

It's important to stress that wise buyers identify and understand what the process looks like, so they're not blindsided by any potential obstacles. Take the time to get the process done thoroughly so that these are not the cause of the delay. If zoning is taken care of, time to closing might be as short as 18 months. Environmental issues will add costs and time. Political setbacks will add more time. Ideally, only buy land that's zoned with the needed infrastructure in place and there's no inherent unknown conditions.

Our big takeaways: the sites that are already zoned, have no environmental conditions, and have adequate infrastructure are the ones that are going to be completed in that 18-month period. The rest will take longer. And a team of professionals assembled ahead of time helps the developer both understand, and successfully navigate, the many complexities.

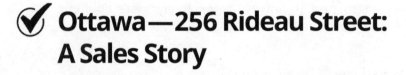

Ottawa—256 Rideau Street: A Sales Story

Challenge

Land is generally the most difficult asset class to sell. There are no assets on the land and there's a zoning process and approvals to worry about. In addition, land acquisition always costs a great deal and takes a long time.

Land is even more difficult to sell when in a non-primary asset class. This piece of land was notably close to the University of Ottawa and had been zoned for smaller apartments uniquely suited to students. In effect, the vision had been baked in.

This meant that the end product would have to be student housing—a very small market.

Action

We knew we were capable of selling this property, and approached the owner, KingSett Capital, to make our case. Our experience with them proved we were there when they needed us. We had written feasibility studies and sold student housing for them in the past. Also, over the years, we had sold a large percentage of all the student housing buildings in Canada—the deal was ours to lose.

We got the listing.

Result

The detailed package we produced had to clearly articulate the vision to the City of Ottawa, the University of Ottawa, and potential buyers, proving that this specific location was ideal for purpose-built student housing—we were selling a vision, not an existing building. In response, we received multiple offers, ranging from $500,000 to about $10 million—an extreme range based on the potential buyer's intended usage.

Developer Ashcroft Homes bought the site.

Testimonial: Scott Coates, KingSett Capital

 In the past, KingSett and our clients have used Derek and his company for feasibility studies, student housing projects, and land sales. When the time came for us to sell this high-density urban site, located close to a university, his firm was the logical choice to broker the deal.

The property achieved a good price, and we transacted. Derek's team continues to help us evaluate lending decisions today.

Street view   Front entrance

Figure 5.3 - Ottawa - 256 Rideau Street

Intensifying Existing Developments

Introduction

Housing prices remain stable, or in some cases, undergo significant increases regardless of the macroeconomic conditions as demand outstrips supply. As a result of that in addition to a changing long-term economic landscape, retail intensification is gaining momentum. By intensifying an existing development with rental apartments, asset developers are weatherproofing their portfolios against future adversity.

Many of our clients are shopping center owners. They traditionally have built retail but now are beginning to consider building apartments. This is especially true today—after experiencing a period of marketplace turbulence. But the reality is that 90 percent of retail developers still think retail is their primary focus in a mixed-use development. In truth, 90 percent of their revenue will come from the residential space.

Retail intensification is the future for this asset class.

Once retail developers shift their focus, the new reality is eye-opening.

The Mindset Challenge

Many reading this book are condominium developers and/or home builders. Because of previous successes in building those condos and homes, the temptation to expand or switch to building rental apartments may have been entertained. However, building apartments is different. These buildings are more than just another place to live, and they require a different mindset to build successfully. In the condo and home-building business, a developer's priority is to build the property, sell it, pay taxes owing, and move on. In the rental business, the job is to build, stabilize, finance, and then, keep the property for up to 100 years.

However, not every rental developer keeps their buildings. Merchant apartment builders generally sell off two out of every three buildings they build, pulling the value out of some and keeping others for long-term wealth generation. The point is, if the goal is to sell a building, a steady income must first be established.

Intensification Challenges / Differences

Everything we know about building a multifamily development becomes a little more challenging when engaged in an intensification project. There are more pieces to manage and more parties to work with. The financial modeling is changed because there's now a land component vended into the deal.

The whole process of intensification is more complicated than building on an undeveloped site.

Parking

If the plan is to build over a parking area, the area needs to be replaced with underground parking or a parking deck. If potential tenants feel they are not able to access the parking they require, they will be compelled to rent elsewhere.

Financial Modeling

When intensifying an existing site, the other buildings on the site get more valuable—that's an important thing to keep in mind. It's not just the numbers on the new building being constructed, it's what happens to the rest of the site.

Feasibility Study

The feasibility study becomes more complex simply because it has more moving parts.

Financing

Financing is complicated because the developer is now working with two assets on the same site, where money from the existing site can be freed to build new assets.

Operating Costs

Operating costs are pretty much the same as described in book five of the *Apartment Developer University* series, *A Field Guide to Municipal Taxes and Operating Costs*. However, there will be some shared-use costs that can be spread between the two properties. The developer should be able to bring their operating costs down. For example, if there are 100 existing units, and then, another 100 new units are built, there isn't necessarily a need for two superintendents.

Rents and Amenities

A premium can be placed on the rents because of the on-site amenities. Suppose there's a grocery store downstairs. What is the premium for being able to buy fresh bread without going outside? Or what is the premium for a perfectly located downtown rental building that's next to an office building with frequent transit stopping right at the front door?

Developers have to think of retail spaces as amenities for the residential tenants.

At the design stage, the building decisions should focus on making the retail space an amenity for the residents. Do those amenities somehow frame the building in a more positive light? In short, choose the retail mix carefully.

Sites with Existing Rental

Developing an existing rental site is a golden opportunity—a win in so many ways. There's as much money to be made on the renovation of an old building as there can be made by building a new apartment when the developer considers the untapped upside potential.

Firstly, the land is vended into the deal. Secondly, after completion, there's twice the number of units, if not more. Therefore, there's twice (or more) of the income—which might be used to upgrade the front entrance and enhance the arrival experience for both buildings. Renters from the existing building can now take advantage of the amenities in the new building, consequently helping to push rents higher.

However, keep in mind that an A-Class building cannot be built beside a C-Class building. The C-Class building standards have to be brought up before building (and marketing) starts on the A-Class building.

What developers always forget when considering an intensification project is that some of the money that they make actually comes from the pre-existing building solely because they've fixed up the entire location, improved living conditions, and created a general uplift in the community.

The Intensification Upside

Rentals are bigger, faster, cheaper, and easier than condos:
- Bigger, because they're scalable; there's a huge demand for apartments.
- Faster, because there are no pre-sales: as soon as the developer buys the land, work begins on digging the hole (pending zoning review and site plan approval, which has to be done regardless of intended residential dwelling type).
- Cheaper, because there is no customization: build to one style or spec, just change the kitchen cabinets every second floor, or offer alternative flooring rather than tailoring each unit to each condominium buyer.
- And Easier, because there is no customer until completion, as opposed to condo sales that occur at the beginning and vary based on market price and availability.

Ultimately, condominium housing is a mature industry. We think it may be approaching the end of its cycle. Apartments are a re-emerging asset class at the beginning of their cycle.

However, a developer never has to sacrifice one for the other if they want to build both. If a developer has established a condominium machine, there's no reason to abandon it. They could develop a rental business without a lot of new internal skills by becoming a merchant apartment builder.

Why Is Rental an Attractive Option?

All asset classes except for self-storage and industrial are opportunities for apartment intensification.

Figure 6.1 - Asset Intensification Risks

Apartments are low risk because they have done extraordinarily well for quite a long time, and are, for the most part, recession proof. During the last few downturns, the sector has seen no reduction in value. We think the apartment sector will become even more desirable. It is the ideal intensification sector.

Condominium sites, especially large condo sites with a combination of condos and rental, are also a great opportunity. By building both on one site at once, a condo builder could leverage their condo successes and efficiencies.

Trends Driving Intensification

Due to the unprecedented surge in online shopping, retail is in the midst of a historic shift. It's clear that the percentage of online purchases is going to keep rising, putting brick and mortar establishments in a financially precarious position. Housing supply continues to fall across North America while prices remain relatively high. At the same time, apartments are becoming more valuable, cap rates are dropping, and demand is solid. The percentage of employees working from home on an ongoing basis has risen dramatically and will likely remain far higher than pre-pandemic levels.

Because of these factors, developers see conversion to residential as a path to restore value to nonperforming or underperforming assets and to meet market demand.

Why Intensify Retail?

Additional Pressures on Retail

Economic downturns aren't new—the most recent economic disruption is just an acceleration of what was already in progress. Retail was under intense pressure before the recent surge in online shopping—it's just become worse. Recently, those indicators have improved further with demand rising as well. In less populous centers with smaller malls, those adverse retail indicators are more pronounced than in larger urban centers.

Maintaining Value

Think of a shopping mall as mostly parking with about 25 percent building. Hence, there's plenty of room to build on and plenty of shopping for the residents to take advantage of. The addition of residential will provide existing retailers a built-in pool of consumers.

- To maintain the value of assets over the long-term, retail landlords should look at mining their portfolios for highest and best uses.
- In most cases, intensifying through mixed-use property development is the best option.
- New apartment construction is a key growth driver for REITs and any developer with multiple intensification sites.

Retail Developer Advantages

Firstly, most large retail sites are 75 percent land, likely with excess parking. With excess parking space available, there's no need to have extra money to buy land. Developers can utilize that unrealized potential, and unlock that value. Secondly, retailers have a wealth of development experience. Though not exactly the experience needed to build apartments, many of the skills can be easily transferred. With some guidance and support to fill the gaps in knowledge, shifting focus to build apartments is within reach. Thirdly, strong retailers, mostly public, have the ability to raise funds and deploy the capital needed to build apartments.

Adequate transit is an important part of rental development. A transit hub nearby or as part of the shopping mall is a significant advantage. Strong transit connections are a plus for purpose-built rental and can reduce parking requirements.

Land Prices

Land prices in major markets have gone up significantly. However, for a major retail developer who already owns the land, the land is free in a sense, becoming the developer's equity.

Parking

The opportunity presented by that excess parking land is huge. Lower density sites with excess parking can be consolidated for higher development. Add underground parking or parking decks (significantly cheaper than going underground) to make up the loss. On small sites, it's also possible to tear down part of the mall or an underperforming big box store. However, even when the existing retail cannot be changed, there remains the option to simply build above the unused or oversupplied parking space.

Why Intensify / Convert Hotels and Office Buildings?

Hotels

The hotel business has had some challenges as of late. That gives an innovative developer the chance to build something special by either converting or rebuilding. Hotels in urban areas have been least able to recover occupancy rates post-pandemic, accelerating the trend experienced over the past two decades.

Office Buildings

Underused office space is also a good candidate for intensification. These are often located in prime locations with great transit and plenty of community amenities close by. The pandemic has proven to both business and employees that working from home is not only doable but desirable.

Amenities

Just as retail sites benefit from local amenities, so do downtown hotels and office buildings. Transit is close by, as is shopping and a vibrant nightlife. Hotels and offices outside of the downtown core, while further from transit, have more space for parking and recreation areas.

Benefits and Challenges

Benefits

- Depending on the jurisdiction, a developer might avoid a lengthy approvals process at the entitlement stage.
- While some jurisdictions still prefer developers to integrate office space into residential buildings, we believe there should be an accommodation and allowance for converting that to a more viable use.
- Because the intensification of an existing building is essentially dealing with a brownfield, there's less construction waste, less of an environmental impact, reduced labor time and cost of construction due to existing parking, building core and shell.

- Most importantly, conversions of this kind revitalize neighborhoods and help keep cities looking refreshed and active.

Challenges

- The physical structure of an office building can present some unique architectural challenges. Of particular consideration are plumbing and electrical systems, which typically have not been designed for residential configuration. Interior walls will need to be demolished to create spaces that are more appropriate in size, often resulting in long and deep units.
- The existing geometry of the building can be limiting. In some cases, a recalibration of the floor plate is necessary.
- As with every renovation, there's always unknown conditions that may be expensive to remedy.
- Sometimes, intensification is limited by open space and parking requirements, which tend to dictate the scale of development.

After Intensification

Real estate development is becoming more and more sophisticated. In addition, projects take years to work through with multiple partners.

To accurately measure the financial viability of a project, a more sophisticated approach is required. This takes financial modeling a step past the conventional stabilized operating pro forma and looks at the cost of capital over time. By collecting as much information as available and tailoring the model to better align with real-world expected costs and the timeline of a development, we can better identify and represent the actual costs and potential required contingencies that must be planned for.

Intensification projects are usually not something a first-time developer should consider.

It's important to note that a developer is looking for two key results from a financial pro forma. First: the land value created by the project. Initially, the value of land is based on the existing income potential of the site. However, that's expanded with the introduction of new rental product, which adds to the existing land value. Second, a developer is not only capitalizing on the land by selling it. By keeping the property and developing it to the end, they realize more value.

Consider what untapped profit exists above and beyond the existing land and how that may affect the overall portfolio.

Value has now been created for two reasons:
- The developer now has a piece of land that generates more value than it used to, and it is land that is essentially free, as it would have been paid off by the mortgage of the first building.
- The developer has land over and above these two assets. If there is a mortgage, the mortgage remains with the existing buildings, so they have a free and clear piece of land.

That piece of land becomes an asset increase in the developer's portfolio. Or it can be used to secure a loan to carry out the next project or the rest of the soft costs—if done properly before construction kicks in.

Cashing In

At a very high level, the developer has monetized the land. There is a value on that land that didn't exist before an asset was built on top of the land—value that the developer created. In addition, the developer has also improved the existing building(s). In effect, there is a community—one that has much more value than when the project began.

Conclusion

There are many programmatic landowners running businesses. Often hidden within their portfolios is underdeveloped land rife with untapped opportunities.

Rental apartment development is the best opportunity for a developer in North America right now. Apartments have become the darlings of Bay Street, Wall Street, and private investors. The perfect storm is happening right now.

- There's strong renter demand in most jurisdictions.
- There's also strong investor demand.
- Apartments get through tough times better than any other significant asset class.
- Interest rates are extraordinarily low right now.

Even if the economy slows and land costs come down, so do construction costs. This is why we call it a perfect storm.

✅ Cambridge—River's Edge: A Sales Story

Challenge

I have great respect for developers who not only take the risks associated with development, but also, have the vision to see what their projects can ultimately become.

Tricar's owner and founder, Joe Carapella, drove me out to a nondescript site in Cambridge, Ontario, next to the Grand River, and described the 20-story towers he envisioned. It was a shabby industrial site that he saw great things in. But I struggled to see his vision. To me, what makes developers truly great—Carapella being one of them—is the ability to take a vision, what could be instead of what is, and betting the farm to see it realized.

A few years later, I came back to two spectacular towers with wonderful views of the river. The whole area had evolved, becoming more gentrified with high-end rental apartments.

Action

Once their buildings are built and stabilized, developers like to keep their money moving. They make big profits, and take great risks, transforming undeveloped land to stabilized buildings. Once a building is stabilized, the yearly return drops—the profits are lower but stable, and the risks are also low.

Tricar typically did not sell the buildings it built. But when I asked if they had an interest in selling this building—their initial response was that they wanted to hold it. Unless, they said, I could get an extraordinary price from an extraordinary buyer.

We introduced Carapella to Philip Fraser, president of Killam Apartment REIT. Killam's goal was to have a portfolio of the newest apartments in Canada. They had the lowest average apartment age in the country and therefore were a good fit.

The transaction went extraordinarily well, which is often the case with a professional seller and buyer. However, several months into the deal, Fraser mentioned that there was a structural problem with a parapet wall. He was a bit perturbed that this happened so soon after purchase, and the repair estimate was very high—in the order of $250,000.

I knew Joe Carapella well—he's proud of his products. He builds his buildings to keep, not sell, and he expects them to hold up well over time. I called Carapella and told him of the issue. He immediately said he would fix the wall at cost: $60,000. He considered this a builder's warrantee—though unspoken, unwritten, it was there, nonetheless. That's the magic of a great deal between professional buyers and sellers.

Result

A few years later, I reintroduced Killam to Tricar on the sale of 1985 Richmond Street, in London, Ontario. Both parties remembered the wall repair and the manner in which it was resolved. Killam was delighted to buy a building from a quality builder with character. This deal proceeded smoother than the first one.

When there's a good relationship between two parties, when each party steps up to the plate, it allows future deals to move far faster and more smoothly. My role was to introduce the two and build the relationship so the deals they made proceeded smoothly. Of greater importance, after the deal was done, I became more than a broker, facilitating solutions to hurdles as they arose.

The ease in which the second transaction proceeded was the result—the parapet wall issue created the second deal. When it was time for Carapella to sell, I brought in Killam—and Carapella was delighted.

Testimonial: Joe Carapella, Tricar Founder

 We're typically not sellers. But in the few instances we do sell, Derek is the person we contact to get the deal across the goal line. During our 25-year relationship with him and his company, we've come to know that he understands new construction as well or better than anyone in the country.

Testimonial: Philip Fraser, Killam Apartment REIT

 Derek is an excellent multi-residential broker. We have bought more newly constructed buildings from him than any other broker in Canada. His understanding of the sector allows him to connect with the right developers and transact deals faster and more smoothly than most brokers.

Tower one   Tower two

Figure 6.2 - Cambridge - River's Edge

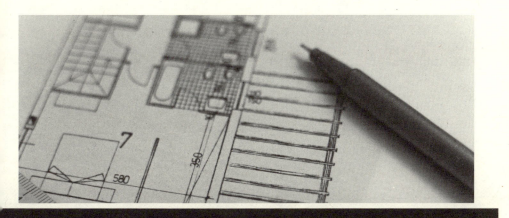

PART 3: Financing the Building

Finding Money

Introduction

To build modern, sophisticated, attractive developments, a developer needs money. That money is raised through financing arrangements a developer makes with lenders or partners, all of whom need to be reassured that the project is viable and attractive to potential renters in its target market.

> *"To make more money, you either make better deals or find cheaper capital."*
> *– Derek Lobo*

Even though this may seem obvious to developers, making a better deal and/or finding cheap capital is not as easy as it sounds. There are the different stages of development of a property to consider, and different ways of financing each one based on risk, potential income, and goals of the parties involved.

When considering their options, developers often ask the following questions:

- What does mezzanine financing look like?
- How do I structure a joint venture (JV)?
- What does take-out financing look like?
- Should I take government incentives when financing?
- How do I build a good relationship with my lender?

This statement summarizes successful financing:
You can bury some of your mistakes if you make them, but you're going to make far fewer mistakes going through this process with an experienced professional.

Development Land

Land is primarily sold to institutional investors or private buyers.

The Institutional Investor

The institutional investor is always on the lookout for land. However, they only have a small percentage of their funds available to buy such land.

They normally want to purchase land that's already properly zoned and shovel-ready. The institutional land loan can be up to 65 percent loan-to-value with a term of two years. Investors do not like to go beyond two years, only doing so in exceptional cases. However, they always want construction to begin within that two-year period.

Institutional buyers want to be a developer's partner. They feel that if they're going to proceed with a land loan and assume some of the risks, they would rather get involved with the construction and exit strategy. The range of interest will likely be prime plus 2 percent to prime plus 2.5 percent.

The Private Buyer

Although perceived negatively, private lenders are not always an unfavorable option. People often think that if they don't qualify for an institutional loan, going private forces them to accept higher interest rates. While that is the case, a private lender serves two purposes that institutional lenders do not address: leverage and flexibility.

Leverage

Firstly, a loan from a private lender can provide more leverage. The private lender will go up to 75 percent loan-to-value instead of the institutional lender's 65 percent. This lets a developer retain more of their equity for construction.

Flexibility

Secondly, private lenders give the developer more timeline flexibility. For example, if a developer is considering purchasing a piece of land that is zoned in the Official Plan as residential and it requires little to no rezoning work, a private lender can provide a bridge loan for two years—and may even give extensions for three to four years as well. There is definitely a market for this kind of flexibility.

For the additional risk carried by a private lender, the developer pays a higher rate—it's 3 to 5 percent above prime depending on individual circumstances. However, this is often offset by the flexibility provided.

Repositioning Existing Multi-residential

Repositioning existing multi-residential is a golden opportunity—a win in so many ways. Firstly, the land is free within the deal. Secondly, once completed, the addition of a second building could double the number of units on a site, if not more. In addition, renters from the existing building can now take advantage of the improved and/or added amenities in the new building, consequently helping to drive rents.

Financing the Repositioning of an Existing Site

Over time, certain properties and developments may become obsolete, perform poorly, or have inherent flaws due to an older design or concept. Communities and local economies also change over time. Industries come and go, demographics shift, and tastes and technology evolve.

To respond to the changing needs of the market, real estate must adapt. Repositioning and/or redevelopment allows landowners, investors, and developers an opportunity to realize greater values from existing sites by replacing, renovating, or repurposing existing properties so they better serve the market and realize greater profits.

There is a great demand for old-stock multi-residential properties. The value exists in the unrealized achievable rents from older tenants who, because of the presence of rent control, pay rents that are significantly below what is currently achievable in the local market. Investors will purchase one of these assets, renovate and reposition it to increase their achievable rents, which in turn increases the property's value and generates a profit. Many investors and property managers have taken this on as their primary investing model and work through these projects systematically.

The key components here are the value of the property and the market rents once a building is stabilized. Provided that everyone is comfortable with those conditions, when the evaluation report comes out, the NOI and resulting property value will take the debt amount to between 70 and 75 percent when CMHC and institutional models are run. In this case, and with that lift, the developer gets the leverage needed for the repositioning.

What the Future Holds

At a very high level, one in every 10 apartment sites can be intensified. In Canada's most populous province, Ontario, there are about 22,000 apartment buildings—potentially 2,200 sites upon which a developer could build on. We can think of those who own existing apartment buildings as joint venture partners. It's a source of land— for them, the land is free. That equity is just sitting there waiting for intensification. We can help them realize that potential.

Many second- or third-generation owners do not have the necessary skills for an intensification project—the properties were built by the first generation and simply handed down. Now, with the markets the way they are, it only makes sense to use that available land as a source of funds to unlock that potential for the benefit of everyone concerned.

Ground-up Multi-residential Construction

Ground-up multi-residential construction financing requires a trusting relationship between the developer and all parties involved. Projects like this require large sums of money, the arrangement probably structured into a junior debt/senior debt situation.

We've said before: for an existing apartment owner, there's trapped equity in the existing property of such value that we can typically give up to 100 percent of the total CapEx required in order to move ahead to construction. Ground-up construction is different.

For ground-up multi-residential construction, there are four financing options open to developers:
1. Banks
2. Mortgage investment groups
3. CMHC (market rental and affordable rental)
4. Private

Of all the important factors that affect financing—and that will really depend upon the debt partner—the most important one is feasibility.

The client needs to be sure that there will be future-market rents on an NOI basis that can support a value, which is going to be equal to or greater than the cost to build. If we give them a positive response, they'll move on to the next step. If that project is not feasible, we may suggest they consider a different parcel of land—if available.

It's important to understand that a lender underwrites the take-out mortgage first. Lenders do that in order to determine the construction mortgage. That's important because it gives us a projection on what the future rental market rates are going to be.

Lenders will still have a subjective opinion as to what they're comfortable with when it comes to probable future rents. As such, this will contribute to a potential lower loan-to-value

(LTV) if the lender pulls back because the NOI is less. If they pull back to a lower loan-to-value at that end, that means the construction loan-to-cost (LTC) is pulled back. Even though the lender offers 75 percent of their loan-to-cost, it would really equate to 65 percent of the budget. Therefore, when a developer enters the institutional market, they must be sure that their partner is on the same wavelength as they are, and that they have a feasibility study ready to support their claims.

Financing

In general, developers either use institutional lenders or private lenders when financing. However, within these two groups, there is some variation. Institutional money includes both government organizations and nonprofit groups. Private lenders include banks, mezzanine lenders, mortgage brokers, and private credit unions.

Government institutions tend to offer the lowest interest rates and longest lending periods but will not typically lend on riskier projects. Private money is more expensive because they can lend on projects that a developer would not otherwise be able to get financing for.

Developer concerns:
- What do they estimate as the value?
- What loan-to-value ratio are they willing to provide?
- What period will the interest rates be for?
- What is the loan repayment period?

The borrower's equity, which translates into net worth, further translates into a guarantee. Equity is very important to lenders, especially in today's market. This will overcome delays, cost overruns, etc., and make sure that the project can be completed. If a developer is experienced (construction experience, that is, has a very strong management record, and a high net worth) there's a very high probability that they'll be able to get decent leverage with low costs.

If their net worth is a little tight, that's still OK. (This is very common if it's their first project, and they've taken all the money they've earned, leaving limited capital. They also may have a line of credit against their home.) In this case, they may be able to find an investment mortgage corporation that's a little more interested because it loves the site. They may already know it's a little riskier, but there's a possibility of arranging a hybrid arrangement with a lender, or a mezzanine lender, that can be made to work for them.

It's important to know that there's a lender for everyone, as long as the developer has a feasible site.

Rate, Term, and Fee Comparison

If a developer's objective is to become wealthy, then they should take out the equity and roll it into their next project. The focus here is not cash flow—they can take the maximum premium because they can also finance that premium. Depending on what their investment horizon is going to look like, the CMHC standard affordable rental is up to 3 percent.

There's currently a big push to get affordable rentals built, with incentives in place to get lower fees but still enjoy great leverage as well as amortization. When financing with multiple sources, the fees between the senior institutions can be combined with the mezzanine lender's fee, making the effective fee about 1 percent plus—to give the developer a little more flexibility.

CONSTRUCTION	CMHC STANDARD (Market Rental)	CMHC STANDARD (Affordable Rental)	BANK OR INSTITUTION	MIC
Loan to Cost	Up to 75%	Up to 95%	Up to 80%	Up to 85%
Interest Rates	~COF + 175-200 (3.10-3.35%)	~COF + 175-200 (3.10-3.35%)	~Prime + 1.00-1.50% (3.95-4.45%)	~Prime + 2.00-4.00%
Term	Up to 2 yrs	Up to 2 yrs	Up to 2 yrs	Up to 2 yrs
Fees	**Application Fees:** • $200 for first 100 units, • $100/unit thereafter (max $55,000) **Premium:** • Up to 5.25% **Lender Proc. Fees for CMHC Standard:** • 0.25-0.50%	**Application Fees:** • $200 for first 100 units, • $100/unit thereafter (max $55,000) **Premium:** • Up to 5.25% **Lender Proc. Fees for CMHC Standard:** • 0.50-0.75%	0.75-1.25%	1.00-1.50%
Guarantee	100%	100%	100%	100%

Figure 7.1 - Rate, Term, and Fee Comparison

The CMHC loan-to-cost is up to 75 percent. However, its brochure says 85 percent. That's because it uses a different cap rate than the market, so it effectively becomes about 75 percent—depending on the underwriting.

Term Financing / Take-out Financing

Financing the construction of a development, or the purchase of a development, requires funds. Typically, those funds come in the form of long-term or short-term financial instruments.

CONSTRUCTION	CMHC STANDARD (Market Rental)	CMHC STANDARD (Affordable Rental)	BANK OR INSTITUTION
Loan to Cost	Up to 85%	Up to 95%	Up to 75%
Interest Rates	~CMB (CDN Mort Bond) = (.79/5yr); (1.07/10yr) CMB + 100	~CMB (CDN Mort Bond) = (.79/5yr); (1.07/10yr) CMB + 100	~5yr BA (SAWP)+175 5yr BA = 1%
Term	Up to 10 years	Up to 10 years	Up to 10 yrs
Fees	**Application Fees:** • $150 for first 100 units, • $100/unit thereafter (max $55,000) **Premium:** • Up to 4.5-5.25% **Lender Processing Fees for CMHC Standard:** • 0.10-0.15% • No fees if rolling construction loan	**Application Fees:** • $150 for first 100 units, • $100/unit thereafter (max $55,000) **Premium:** • Up to 4.5-5.25% **Lender Processing Fees for CMHC Standard:** • 0.10-0.15% • No fees if rolling construction loan	1-15%
Guarantee	After 12 consecutive months of stabilized rent the guarantee can be reduced to 40% of the outstanding loan amount owing under the mortgage from time to time	After rent-up, when the project has achieved the rental income used in the underwriting of the load, the loan may become non-recourse to the borrowers and guarantors	Limited
Amortization	40 years	40 years	30 years
DSCR	1.20 (Term of 10+ years) 1.30 (Term of <10 years)	1.10	1.15-1.25

Figure 7.2 - Term-Take-out Financing

129

CMHC offers resources and funding for new builds, conversions, and renovations.

Our advice, before committing to a loan, is to shop around so you get the best effective rate.

It's also our recommendation that a developer sell a project once it's leased up. That way, the full potential of that project is realized (lending institutions will see it as such), making take-out financing easier and cheaper, since institutions may see that project's value more favorably.

Who Should Finance?

Who should put the long-term financing on the building—the developer or purchaser?

A developer may take on the debt for the long-term financing, qualifying for both a 10-year mortgage from CMHC and a 10-year one from an institution. Later, they may want to have someone else buy the mortgage. But they now risk getting into a situation that the buyer does not meet the criteria necessary to assume the mortgage, thus leaving them holding the property. If they sell the building pre-leased, they lose that risk, as the purchaser will apply for their own financing.

Our advice for developers is to build an apartment building, get it essentially leased up, then sell it. Let the buyer get the financing.

Buyers are sophisticated. They've got good lender relationships and can borrow bigger, faster, cheaper, and easier than a developer can.

The sales process should begin when a building is 30 percent leased up. This allows a developer to prove the rents during the sales process and further increase the overall value of the property. Final sale should only occur when the building is close to stabilization or at approximately 95 percent occupancy. The closer a building is to being fully leased; the more buyer interest a building will garner.

We begin the sales process early to ensure we get solid traction with interested buyers as quickly as possible. This gives us time to complete due diligence, then close the sale by the time lease-up is nearing its final stages.

Conclusion

It's probably true that everyone looks for easy formulas and truisms that simplify financing. The reality is that it's not that simple.

> *The overriding factor, however, is quite simple: "Are you building to keep or are you building to sell?"*

This will determine how a building will be financed, the unit sizes and mix, and the risks a developer is willing to take. But keep in mind that if the intention is to keep a building for 25 years, it will be a great investment no matter how it was initially financed.

Financing is an entirely different part of the business. The person who raises the equity, finds the mezzanine financing, and gets the financing arranged is not necessarily the person who builds the building. We've seen some very interesting second-generation families who have become builders: one family member gravitating toward the development side, another to the property management side, and yet, another to the financial side.

Financing requires a different skill set. Negotiating with a drywall contractor is not the same as finding an equity partner. If a developer brings the same approach to hiring a contractor as they bring to finding an equity partner, they're not going to find one. There's a very interesting dynamic that goes on between borrowers and lenders, and relationships are built that last years. Over time, many deals get made between a lender, builder, and those who facilitate those kinds of negotiations.

We've had long-lasting relationships with many different parties, to the point where they come to us when they need deals to work. There's a huge trust factor that comes into play, where the facts are brought out (no matter how ugly), and the issues hammered out in good faith, all with an eye to actually getting the job done. Working with trusted partners eliminates a lot of guesswork and uncertainty. When we're working with an institution, we're not guessing what they can and cannot do—we're submitting a debt structure that they're thinking of bidding on, and then, we continue to work with the parties until the project is complete.

That lender becomes the developer's partner throughout the project's construction—there will be challenging situations along with good times. We want to ensure that there's a meeting of the minds throughout the whole process. That, to us, is extremely important.

Kitchener—Collegeview Commons: A Sales Story

Challenge

Our client, Drewlo Holdings, the single largest private apartment developer in Canada, has built a development machine over the decades that produces two to three apartments a year in southwestern Ontario.

Their goal was to diversify into student housing, a subset of apartments. To that end, they retained us to acclimatize them to this asset class.

Action

Since Canadian student housing was still in its early stages, I took Mr. Eugen Drewlo and his son, Allan, to East Lansing, Michigan, to tour several cutting-edge student housing buildings at the University of Michigan.

What the Drewlos saw amazed them. It was like a view into the future. There, student housing is a primary industry in a functioning investment marketplace, with financiers, merchant student housing developers, and institutions all doing business together in a mature market. We introduced them to the important players and consultants in the marketplace so they would know how to replicate this model in Canada.

The trip inspired the Drewlos.

Result

Drewlo Holdings had purchased a site near Conestoga College in Kitchener. Fresh from their experience at the University of Michigan, they boldly built a 250-unit, two-tower apartment community with 1,000 beds. It was amazing to see a developer in their first foray into student housing build the largest student housing facility in Canada.

After a number of years of successful ownership, they decided that they didn't want to be in the student housing business any longer. Drewlo Holdings listed the building for sale with Rock Advisors and we transacted in May 2019.

Because they trusted me when they were building the building, I had earned the right to sell it for them.

Testimonial: Allan Drewlo, Drewlo Holdings

We knew Derek very well since my family had been working with him for 30 years. He had carved out a great reputation in student housing and new apartment construction. So, when we thought of moving into the student housing asset class, he was our natural first call.

After he'd given us his opinion of the sector and the advantages it offered, we proceeded to build Collegeview Commons in Kitchener.

As you know, student housing is a viable asset class for apartment developers, but it requires a different management platform. In this case, Derek helped us retain a platform manager that did a wonderful job until the decision was made to sell the asset in 2019.

At that point, Derek was our first choice to serve as broker, successfully selling the building for us.

Exterior view   Street entrance

Figure 7.3 - Kitchener - Collegeview Commons

Building with a Joint Venture Partner

Introduction

Apartment projects are capital intensive, needing more money than the average condo of the same value. When additional capital is needed, creating a joint venture (JV) is a possible solution.

This collaboration of two or more parties (the transaction's sponsor, developer or owner, and investor or investors) pools both cash and talent to financially enable and operationally execute a real estate transaction. Fundamentally, a JV is more than just numbers and formulas. It's about a close and open relationship between the developer and the partners. This communication will determine the joint venture's structure and the ease in which it progresses.

Our team's years of experience with joint partnerships and extensive business relationships are indispensable resources. While working together, the parties still maintain their own business identity and responsibilities, with profits assigned in whatever way is best for a particular project, and form relationships that last a lifetime.

Motivations

The developer's motivations for entering into a joint venture are these:

- The passion to build apartments
- The need to have a partner who has experience building or funding apartment projects
- A partner who will share the risks
- A need to maintain some liquid capital by finding alternative sources of equity for their project
- The drive to learn as they proceed
- The desire to build and/or strengthen relationships

From the investor's point of view, a competent developer can fill in the missing pieces in their quest to build apartments. Investors have:

- The passion to build apartment buildings
- The desire to remain a passive partner
- The need to expand their portfolio beyond existing stock
- The desire to invest in a market with a proven track record

Advantages and Risks

There are several advantages all parties to a joint venture will enjoy:

- The investment, or initial capital, is shared between the parties.
- Some expenses can be shared, reducing overall costs.
- The technical and financial expertise is shared, making the joint venture stronger than its parts.
- New markets can be considered when relevant local knowledge may benefit the venture.
- New or more diverse revenue streams can be considered.

- Overall market credibility can be enhanced.
- Competitive pressures can be met successfully.

However, there are some risks associated with joint ventures. Chief among those:

- Failure to initially communicate and define clearly overall objectives can strain relationships as time goes on
- Poor cooperation or cultural mismatches will threaten a relationship
- Failure to define at onset the roles expected will result in one party feeling taken advantage of, leading to problems

The Three Questions

Typically, when we are structuring joint ventures, we've already done the feasibility study for the project. We've brought the developer up to speed, that is, we've made them an apartment scientist and we've put a package together. At this point, the investor will need some fundamental questions answered.

Note that it's a misconception that the deal comes first and foremost. Relationships and goals are vitally important—in some cases they are the driving factor.

1. Who Is the Developer?

What potential JV partners are most interested in has nothing to do with property or location; it's about the developer's credibility, integrity and reputation, and presence in the marketplace.

The pertinent questions for a developer to ask of their own business are:

- What is my perception of the marketplace?
- What is my history?
- What are my contingency plans?

A developer needs to be able to answer these thoroughly if they intend to build apartments with a partner. If the story presented is not right, they are never going to get to the point of discussing an actual deal. Some large developers with quite attractive deals, lots of land, and the competence to build apartments have been unable to find partners simply because their reputation was less than stellar. The opportunity to describe where or what the potential deal might be was lost.

The developer's integrity and reputation are critical. Often, the first meeting between a JV partner and an equity source is not in a meeting room; it's touring an apartment built previously since that shows the potential partner what kind of work the developer has done. Sometimes the first meeting is an informal lunch where the two parties simply get to know one another. The getting down to the business of numbers is done later, after an understanding and a sharing of goals has been established.

2. Where Is the Deal?

Institutional partners often operate in specific geographical areas. If a developer wants to build in a solid mid-market but that location is not where a potential JV partner wants to work, they're not going to go to their credit committee and try and sell the deal.

Though investors prefer proven markets, there may be many markets nearby that are great to build in. For example, would they consider Laval, just outside of Montreal? Or, might they consider Bethesda, outside of Washington, DC. Some of these secondary markets are wonderful opportunities for developers. They may not be on the investor's checklist, but they may go ahead if they think the deal is worthwhile and the developer is someone they can trust.

3. What is the Deal?

Building apartments is very capital intensive. As a result, the developer needs a JV partner at the top of the capital stack—the highest risk location. What the deal is comes down to details: the finances, the feasibility study, the time frame, and much more.

Risk and Relationship

To a great degree, risk and relationships are closely associated. Individuals or groups are more likely to accept greater risks if they're working with someone they respect and trust. The partnership accepts the risks together, knowing the others will do their utmost to see the project through successfully.

Risk Tolerance

What is risk tolerance and how does it affect a deal—for both parties? The life stage of each party influences all deals. An investor group member will have a different way of looking at the world at age 70 than they will at 45. Are they considering divestment plans? What are their expansion plans? What are their plans for estate planning? This all ties into their long-term objectives.

Basically, understand where the risk/reward future lies in the business.

Communication Is Key

The important lesson to learn is that, besides the numbers, a deal is like a marriage—it's the relationship between the parties that comes first and foremost, even before a deal is discussed. Frequent and open communication is vital. Potential partners need to walk through existing buildings, meet face-to-face, and maintain frank communication. But the effort is worth it. The relationship they build is going to help them make a lot of money together.

The Developer's Position Within a JV

A developer must be fully prepared with a complete package and a firm understanding of what the lender's needs are.

Our feasibility study should be the first thing shown. After all, it's those details that first convinced them what and where they should build. These proved how much rent could be charged, the depth of the market, and how much money they stood to make when sold, or kept, if they so prefer. A developer must then put all that data into a framework using a detailed financial model and present a complete package that describes them, the market, and the deal.

In book six of the *Apartment Developer University* series, *The Four Factors that Drive Rent*, we covered what market rent levels are and how a developer determines setting their own rents. A potential JV partner, a financial expert, will know what those numbers mean and how to translate them into a bottom line.

Investor Group Expectations

A joint venture will usually be managed by the managing general partner (MGP) while the investor group (IG) takes on a more passive role.

The investor group will seek active returns on a development with little or no involvement. They're looking for returns higher than they're going to get at the bank for five-year GICs or 10-year bonds.

The investor group does not offer personal guaranties. They seek a safety-first return of equity within a three- to seven-year time frame. And they seek a safety-first interest rate based on bank prime plus 3 to 5 percent. That can be modified a bit depending on the formula structure. Even though in most cases the investor understands the business and historically has been in a managing partner's shoes before, they normally don't want to be involved in the daily management of the deal. But rest assured, they do understand the business.

An investor group seeks reversionary ownership interest from 33 to 66 percent. The percentage depends on the managing general partner's equity contribution and position regarding recoveries of the managing general partner's said equity. An investor group works on an internal rate-of-return formula. They're concerned with their risk-reward position. They have other places to invest their money in. That could be in a business, the stock market, or in other development opportunities. Our job is to show, or substantiate, why an investor should invest in our development at the expense of the other opportunities they may have. Typically, that takes the form of an IRR over a period of time.

The experience of investors is that apartment returns are typically lower than pre-pandemic retail development. It's up to us to help them understand that apartment returns have far less volatility, much better financing, and more liquidity than other assets.

Remember, apartments are the greatest long-term investments over time.

MGP Components

The managing general partner has different roles.

Figure 8.1 - MGP Roles

The graphic does not depict five different partners taking on the managing partner's duties—it's to illustrate that there's more than just one aspect to the job. In the past, it was thought that anyone who was a managing general partner took on all of these roles. Things are more complicated today, necessitating the need for a managing partnership made up of two to five individuals, each of whom brings a complementary skill set to that managing general partner.

We know that in today's business world, an individual cannot be an expert in all areas—it's far better to be skilled in one area and bring that to the table in order to complement the skills of the others.

The Finder

This individual locates the opportunity and presents it to the managing general partnership, and then, receives the acquisition through the close of the purchase.

The Funder

The funder is responsible for bringing in the investor group equity.

The Administrator

The administrator is the behind-the-scenes person responsible for ongoing administration work, written reports to the investor group, bank, bookkeeping, tax preparation functions, etc.

The Coordinator

The coordinator manages the day-to-day details of the construction and sees the idea through to completion. They are the primary contact person for all project activities once the project is underway.

The Loan Guarantor

Finally, the loan guarantor is the person, or persons, with sufficient financial strength who puts their financial statement at risk to guaranty construction financing, take-out financing, etc.

MGP and IG Responsibilities

Both the managing general partner and investment group have their own set of responsibilities.

MGP Responsibilities

It's critical that the MGP complete a well-thought-out, thorough, investment package. An investor is going to expect them to leave something behind they can refer to that will expand and support their claims. Producing a package that leaves investors wanting for information or guessing is counterproductive. We have written these documents for years. We know what investors expect and what developers should provide so that they get the right message across.

If a developer is serious about raising funds from reliable, reputable investors, then the developer should go through the trouble of getting this documentation done professionally.

Value

An investor package is going to be quite substantial and designed to go through many people's hands. A folder with a few loose sheets of charts and a bio inside will not cut it. Investors want to know everything—in detail. The managing general partner's goal is to always add more value than they get back.

Integrity

This document is a reflection of the developer. If the investor is pleased by what they see—and might even invest—they will pass the document along to other investors. It's a referral of sorts. The document becomes part of the developer's track record—their reputation. Make sure it reflects integrity and thoroughness.

Communication

It's difficult to stress this enough: communicate, communicate, communicate! Never leave things undone or unsaid. Be open and available.

Bad News First

One thing that we've always known and stressed: bad news should be delivered immediately; good news can wait. The last thing a developer wants is investors getting some bad news from a third party.

Share

A developer needs to share their knowledge and tell their investors why they're doing what they're doing. The more investors know about them, the better they will feel.

Review and Renew

A developer needs to review and renew their goals. They need to be ready for change and be open to communicating those changes to their investors.

Counsel

A developer should be prepared to counsel their joint venture partners when it's necessary to do so, with the provision that investors can do the same to them, if necessary. Both can learn from this. However, the developer is running the project, and investors have to be aware that they can run it competently.

Listen First

Listen first, talk second. Investors will want to talk with developers. So let them say what they feel they need to say.

Be Fair

The developer must be fair to both the investor group and to themselves. Since apartments do well in poor economies, both developer and investor will weather those challenges well. Focus on relationships; keep them alive and productive.

Also important, we think, is to have some fun. You don't want this to be a stressful situation. With everyone on the same page, worry should be reduced.

IG Responsibility

The investor group has responsibilities as well as the MGP.

Leave the MGP Alone

Most importantly, let the managing general partner do their job effectively and make unencumbered business decisions. The IG should not interfere. An IG comes to the deal because it's a good one, and with a sound development organization behind it—let it do what it knows best.

Partner with Common Goals

Only partner with MGPs who share your goals. This ensures that everyone is aligned and has similar investment strategies. In the event of a challenging situation, the IG can be sure that the MGP's response will be the same as how they would respond. This bolsters confidence and mitigates risk to some extent because the investor knows that issues will be dealt with appropriately. The IG can only find those things out by getting involved, communicating, and understanding MGP goals. When they're both going in the same direction, business will proceed smoothly.

Investor Group Money Is Cheap

We've all heard the expression that they who have the money have the gold. We might challenge that by saying money is fairly cheap now—it's the people who add the real value in a project.

> *Talent is where the value lies. Money is just a tool needed to help realize those profits.*

A developer should never overlook an investor's goals when they offer their investment. Although money is gold, it comes with strings attached, which can significantly impede the ability to complete a project and react to circumstances in the way a developer expects without pushback from the investors. Financing can be found relatively cheaply. A developer might want to consider another IG partner if goals are not aligned— an IG should add value to a developer's project, resulting in a higher return. The people they do business with should be those who will help bring better returns in the long run, not those always searching for that quick, big deal.

Relationships First

Before we get into the details of the different structures, we need to step back a bit to focus on the relationships between the various parties. It really comes down to waiting until everyone has determined each other's sensitivities and goals so the structure can take these into account.

For developers, a word of caution. We have a saying in this business that asserts that some of these investors eventually want to lend-to-own. A weak developer should be wary that when working with a cash-rich investor, they may be in a position to take over and end up in the developer's position.

Progression of a JV Partnership

Over the duration of a joint venture, relationships change as progress is being made, sort of like a football game, but with both sides winning.

However, be patient. Though everyone wants to throw a touchdown pass, progress is usually just a few yards at a time. It's best if all parties know this in advance so that the tendency to rush through is avoided, and everyone feels they've been heard and understood at all times. The project is not going to make it across the finish line overnight—but it will get there!

Like a football game's quarters, there are different stages of progress during negotiation and different mindsets within each to be aware of. The first quarter is going to look very different from the second quarter, or the third. And hopefully, the last quarter, the one that crystallizes what everyone had dreamed all along, is the one supported by all the research.

One of the biggest reasons that joint venture's fall apart is the mindset that says that once large sums of money are taken up front, the deal is effectively closed. After all, the money is in the developer's hands—they may feel like they can move on to the next deal. No, they cannot! The deal is not over until it's finalized. The developer should take their time. They should move the deal forward in increments, shift mindsets at each phase change, and know that though some parts of the deal are done, more remains.

What a JV Looks Like

A joint venture is not like a purchase or sale agreement, or a rental study. In general, those all look the same.

Joint ventures are all different.

We've done a joint venture where the entire transaction, one worth $250 million, took 40 pages—very short by JV standards. The reason for the brevity: there had been ongoing trust between the buyer and seller developed over a series of meetings. Another JV deal, this one for just $70 million, was far different. Buyer and seller were never fully on the same page. Everything had to be documented, and every alternative explored and written out. That document cost $500,000. When an unanticipated scenario presented itself, the process quickly dissolved into conflict.

There is really no shortcut. A developer spends the time to get a thorough feasibility study done so they can build the right product for the marketplace. A JV partnership should be approached with the same thoroughness. When there's a high level of trust and an equally high level of competency, the process will proceed far more smoothly than anticipated.

Solid relationships created in a joint venture will serve all parties well. Once everyone is on the same page, the parties can build the right JV structure for that deal and circumstance for everyone's benefit.

JV Structures

How does a developer structure a deal mathematically? There are three major forms: Pref and Promote, Traditional Split, and Waterfall.

Beyond those three, there's the Back End Promote, where the promoter (developer or owner) is incentivized with a large percentage of the profit dependent on exceeding certain agreed-to hurdles, and many different deal-based variations of the other forms. Since compensation is a key ingredient of any JV agreement, the parties can devise a host of variations based on a specific transaction, the market, capital as a whole, investment percentage, risk profile of the project, and/or the efforts of the parties involved.

The **Pref** is a priority return on cash invested, the **Promote** is an additional share of profits granted to the sponsor above and beyond their pro rata cash invested, and the **Waterfall** is a fancy way of providing a successively larger promote to the sponsor, the better the transaction performs. In this way, the sponsor has a financial incentive to pay close attention and strive to outperform for the life of the transaction.

Pref and Promote

This is an example of an investment in an existing income-producing building. ("Pref," or preferred, is stated as a percentage.)

Transaction Brief

PROPOSAL: Investment produces the following equity cash flow

PARTNERSHIP: Partner with an Equity Investor who injects 90% of equity

INITIAL EQUITY INVESTMENT: $1,000,000

PROJECT DURATION: 5 years

CASH FLOW

CF0	($1,000,000)
CF1	$80,000
CF2	$83,000
CF3	$102,000
CF4	$118,000
CF5	$142,000 + $1,450,000

Pref and Promote Model

	INVESTOR	PROMOTER	TOTAL	
Investment Amount	$900,000	$100,000	$1,000,000	
Investment %	90%	10%	100%	
1st Preferred Return	8%	-		Then if excess remains
2nd Preferred Return	-	8%		Then if excess remains
Split Balance in Ratio of	70%	30%		Note the Promote to Promoter

Upon Sale
Return Principal first
Then pay Preferred Return
Then split the balance in ratio of split

Figure 8.2 - Pref and Promote

Upon sale, the principal is returned first, with an excess percentage paid to the investor. If more excess exists, the deal pays the promoter a preferred return. If some remains, then the balance is split in the ratio of the split. The promoter (developer) stands to make a greater return on their money than the investor, even if the absolute amounts are greater for the investor (because the investor has a very high percentage of the equity). The promoter is well compensated for a job well done.

Traditional Split

Transaction Brief

THE DEAL: Develop Apartment Building in a Suburban Location and Sell to Pension Fund

TOTAL PROJECT COST: $115,000,000
DEBT: $81,000,000   70%
EQUITY: $34,000,000   30%

PARTNERSHIP: Partner with an Equity Investor who injects 70% of equity

PROJECT DURATION: 2 years (for simple calculations in model) - typical duration is 3-5 years

DEBT BALANCE ($ CURVE): $85,100,623 on closing @5% interest

PROJECT NOI: $7,750,000 representing 6.7% Development Yield

PROJECTED EXIT CAP: 5.5%

PROJECTED SALE PRICE: $140,909,091

Traditional Split Model

	EQUITY PARTNER	DEVELOPER	TOTAL	
Equity	70%	10%	100%	
Equity Investment	$23,800,000	$10,200,000	$34,000,000	
1st Preferred Return	10%	-		Then if excess remains
2nd Preferred Return	-	7%		Then if excess remains
Split Balance in Ratio of	70%	30%		Note the Promote to Promoter

Upon Sale
Return Principal first
Then pay Preferred Return
Then split the balance in ratio of split

Figure 8.3 - Traditional Split

Upon sale: the deal returns principal first, then pays a preferred return to the investor. The excess (lower percentage) goes to the developer; the remainder is split (in the equity ratio). There is no promote to the developer. In this case, the investor stands to make a higher percentage than the developer.

Waterfall

Transaction Brief

THE DEAL: Develop Apartment Building in a Suburban Location and Sell to Pension Fund

TOTAL PROJECT COST: $115,000,000
DEBT: $81,000,000 70%
EQUITY: $34,000,000 30%

PARTNERSHIP: Partner with an Equity Investor who injects 70% of equity

PROJECT DURATION: 2 years (for simple calculations in model) - typical duration is 3-5 years

DEBT BALANCE ($ CURVE): $85,100,623 on closing @5% interest

PROJECT NOI: $7,750,000 representing 6.7% Development Yield

PROJECTED EXIT CAP: 5.5%

PROJECTED SALE PRICE: $140,909,091

IRR Waterfall Model

Sale Price	$140,909,091
Cost of Sale	$1,409,091
Loan Repayment	$85,100,623
Cash to Distribute	**$54,399,377**
Equity Partner Capital	$23,800,000
Developer Capital	$10,200,000

Invested Capital to be returned first

IRR WATERFALL AGREEMENT		EQUITY PARTNER	DEVELOPER
IRR up to	15.00%	70%	30%
IRR from/to	15.01% - 20.00%	65%	35%
IRR from/to	20.01% - 25.00%	60%	40%
IRR from/to	25.01% +	55%	45%

Figure 8.4 - Waterfall

The waterfall model has an upside to the developer that is linked to achievement of IRR on the project. Percentages are arranged initially. The higher the IRR, the more the developer makes.

Waterfall Versus Traditional Split

Waterfall Versus Traditional Split Payout

Sale Price	$140,909,091	Assuming Exit Price at a Cap of 5.50%
Cost of Sale	$1,409,091	
Loan Repayment	$85,100,623	
Cash to Distribute	**$54,399,377**	

Equity Partner Capital	$23,800,000	Invested Capital to be returned first
Developer Capital	$10,200,000	

Waterfall

IRR WATERFALL AGREEMENT		EQUITY PARTNER	DEVELOPER
IRR up to	15.00%	70%	30%
IRR from/to	15.01% - 20.00%	65%	35%
IRR from/to	20.01% - 25.00%	60%	40%
IRR from/to	25.01% +	55%	45%

PARTNER'S CASH FLOW - WATERFALL		EQUITY PARTNER	DEVELOPER	TOTAL
Waterfall Cash Flows	CF0	($23,800,000)	($10,200,000)	($34,000,000)
	CF1	-	-	-
	CF2	$37,272,157	$17,127,220	$54,399,377
IRR		25.14%	29.58%	26.49%

Traditional

TRADITIONAL AGREEMENT	EQUITY PARTNER	DEVELOPER	TOTAL
1. Equity Pref. Return	10%	-	
2. Developer Pref. Return	-	7%	
3. Split	70%	30%	

PARTNER'S CASH FLOW - TRADITIONAL		EQUITY PARTNER	DEVELOPER	TOTAL
Traditional Cash Flows	CF0	($23,800,000)	($10,200,000)	($34,000,000)
	CF1	-	-	-
	CF2	$38,544,378	$15,854,999	$54,399,377
IRR		27.26%	24.68%	26.49%

Figure 8.5 - Waterfall Versus Traditional Split

Five percent is a lot of motivation for a developer. The small relative decrease for the investor is not as big a change. For higher achievements, the developer's percentage goes even higher.

Summary

The best model split for the parties is the waterfall model. Under the traditional model, the developer would get 40 percent IRR assuming the amazing $155 million sale price. If the parties had structured a waterfall model, the IRR would be 51 percent. The developer's 11 percent increase significantly motivates the developer to work in the best interests of the project.

At the same time, the equity partner's return has not materially changed. Their returns are 5 percent down when compared to the other model, but they are left in a very good position, as 37 percent IRR is still substantial. If a developer is capable, their ability to receive a handsome profit is quite achievable. But first and most importantly, they need to get the rent right.

Rents determine profits. It's also something a developer controls, which in effect gives them control over their profits.

Conclusion

If a developer is going to be involved in a joint venture, they've got to give their partner a comfort level that goes beyond the paperwork. What the investor is buying is a developer's skill set to build the apartment and manage all the moving parts.

Though some of a developer's potential partners may have been in the game for quite some time and have proven track records, things do change. Technology changes, as do financial conditions. Much like the emergence of the scientist developer, JV partnerships have become much more of a science.

> *The way decisions are made are less gut feeling and more big data.*

However, relationships still matter as much as they ever have. Time spent on the relationship side of any deal will pay off dividends over a full career—invest heavily and wisely and the developer will enjoy the fruits of their efforts.

Ottawa—151 Greenbank Road: A Sales Story

Challenge

Phoenix Developments president, Cuckoo Kochar, an experienced financial individual, was now one of Ottawa's largest developers. He hired us to do a feasibility study on one of his first apartment buildings—151 Greenbank Road.

We got the listing early in the construction phase. Traditionally, it's very difficult for a buyer to buy an apartment that's not yet completed and has unproven rents. A buyer wants stability, and the developer cannot give the buyer that yet. Developers want to make a profit (high profit with high risk) over a short period of time; buyers want steady income over a long period of time. During the transition, there's uncertainty.

What was needed was an understanding between developer and buyer of the existing conditions. Yet, the timing made it more difficult because of the uncertainty around the value of the building.

To dissipate that uncertainty, the developer must show the buyer that the building is being leased at the proper rate (say, without incentives), and with the right closing ratio. Our role is to transfer to the buyer the confidence that the building will get fully leased and help the seller get the building fully leased at the highest achievable rent. Because we are leasing experts, we can credibly do this.

Action

We had a number of qualified buyers come through the building, but they were unable to get a transaction done. Once the leasing began, we brought in a proven buyer, Killam Apartment REIT.

Killam Apartment REIT understood the new construction business. They had bought several buildings from us before and were developers themselves. This gave them an added edge because they understood what a developer goes through.

Result

Early in the lease-up phase, Killam REIT put in an offer. As they continued through their due diligence process, leasing continued. The leasing success indicated a good rental trend and where the market actually was. Killam REIT was comfortable moving forward with a firm deal before the building was fully stabilized.

The deal was structured so both parties were rewarded for getting the leasing done faster and achieving high rents.

Testimonial: Cuckoo Kochar, Phoenix Developments

 Our plan is to enter the apartment development business this decade in a significant way. Fortunately, we had been introduced to Derek by another developer. So, we knew of him and his company, and reputation, long before this transaction.

We retained him to do several feasibility studies for us, including the feasibility study for 151 Greenbank Road, Ottawa. He is the natural broker for the buildings we build, part of an ongoing relationship we have with him, utilizing his professional teams from feasibility, design, construction, to lease-up and finally brokerage.

Figure 8.6 - Ottawa - 151 Greenbank Road

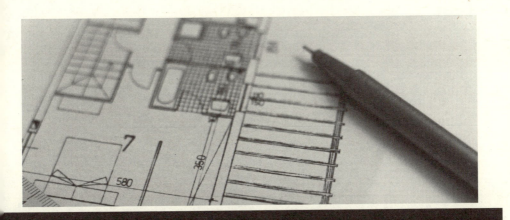

PART 4: Filling Up
the Building

The
Marketing Plan

Introduction

Writing and executing a detailed and comprehensive marketing and operating plan is vital. Fundamentally, marketing is part of the foundation of what a developer does if they're a merchant apartment builder.

> *Begin your marketing plan on day one because marketing is really where the money gets made.*

A development's marketing plan should be set up the same way a developer has set up their construction budget—from day one, using a Gantt chart to outline all the steps required based on the date and stage of development, and end only when the building is stabilized or sold. Moreover, the plan should be supported by a talented team of professionals to execute each of the steps under a developer's guidance.

Every marketing plan is different. Plans are tailored to create market awareness, generate buzz, and ultimately, get the highest rents possible. A downtown building with a younger professional renter profile demographic from 25 to 45 is going to be very different from a suburban building where people are selling their homes before moving in.

Understanding the Renter

Developing renter personas is one of the most crucial steps in developing a marketing plan. By understanding who the residents are going to be, the developer can better design a building to suit them, tailor an appealing message, and develop marketing that targets them specifically.

A renter persona (profile) takes detailed demographic data and lays it out in a way that is easily digestible for decision-making. Specifically, a developer needs to know:
- potential renters' age and life stage;
- their income and spending patterns;
- how they think;
- what their values are;
- their media consumption patterns;
- their typical oppositions and objections; and
- details based on specific markets and local circumstances.

Renter profiles determine how and where a developer markets. Although a majority of marketing is conducted online, a significant amount of data is generated using conventional marketing methods and physical media. The degree to which each advertising medium is used will depend on the target renter and the specific market.

Marketing Is an Ongoing Process

We've witnessed dramatic changes in the markets over the last five years—housing prices have gone up quickly. This increase drove prices higher than some segments of the market could afford. In addition, some market demographics changed more quickly than anticipated. In this atmosphere, marketing becomes far more important.

Once the building is stabilized, there is some breathing space. However, once units start turning over—depending on location and unit mix this can be as high as 30 percent of the units—they will require yearly re-leasing. At this point, the marketing plan, though ramped down somewhat from the early hectic days, still has a valuable role to play. In essence, it never stops.

Types of Marketing Plans

There are three types of marketing plans. Each is specifically tailored to each phase—construction, lease-up, or stabilized—with different goals in mind.

1. Development and Construction

At the very beginnings of the development process, begin generating community awareness and market presence. There likely will be some local awareness just because a new project is beginning. However, reaching out into the community draws the attention of those who may be interested in renting as opposed to the general public.

2. Active Lease-up

The most active phase is during the building's lease-up phase. The plan's main focus is to draw potential tenants into the building. The effort expended at this point is enormous. All those interested in renting must be first reached, and then, convinced that the building is the place to live, and, because of the quality of the building's features, worth the high rents being charged.

3. Stabilized

The stabilized marketing plan is designed to maintain a marketing presence and to continually keep the building full after 95 or 98 percent occupancy has been reached.

Those three marketing phases work the same whether the developer is planning to keep the building or sell. However, for the merchant apartment builder, the focus is to sell the building before it's full in order to help alleviate the costs associated with carrying expensive financing.

Developer Differences

When we first meet a developer, we first want to know if the building will be kept or sold. Many design decisions are based on the developer's intent. Decisions about the leasing process are also affected.

We also want to know what type of apartment leaser the developer is. The attitude around rent pricing and marketing depends on the developer's personality and investment goals, appetite for risk, and the reality of the marketplace at that time and place. We tailor our marketing and rental strategy based on the personality of the developer—but the strategy may evolve due to situation or goal changes.

Leasing Personalities

There are five overarching personalities:
- The Balanced Pricer: This is the set-it-and-forget-it developer.
- The Occupancy Defender: The name says it all— this is a conservative person.
- The Rent Driver: The rent driver wants a good, and sometimes quick, return.
- The Vacancy Allergic: This developer type just wants to get the building full and will forgo rent increases in favor of stability.
- The Lease-upper: A temporary state of mind, usually found in the middle of leasing.

Knowing the above and the associated end goals allow us to create a leasing and marketing strategy that matches the developer's personality and goals. It enables us to get as close to market-leading rents as possible while still being sensitive to the developer's needs.

Targeting the Right Renters

Finding out who the target renter is and getting to understand them well enough to be able to design a building for them, is really an extension of the feasibility study. These renter personas represent the typical renter households found in new, high-quality rental buildings. They range in life stage, achievable incomes, tenure, and unit preferences, meaning that each requires not only a different unit type, but also, a unique leasing strategy.

Urban Singles

The urban singles are typically between the ages of 20 and 34. In a suburban market, they are between 25 and 34.

They're unmarried, recently graduated young professionals, and living on their own making strong incomes. They prefer one-bedroom units.

Professional Couples

They're between 25 and 34, recently graduated, and earn high incomes. They usually prefer two-bedroom units with incorporated office space.

Downsizers

Aged 45 to 60, they typically reside in single-family homes, empty now because their children have moved away. They're looking to downsize and reduce the amount of money and time they spend on maintenance. Older downsizers are often interested in the largest of the available two-bedroom units as they require a greater amount of space to store a lifetime of collected possessions.

Divorced Singles

Divorced singles are an excellent source of potential renters. They've likely moved from single-family homes and are now in a position where they can't afford to buy because of circumstances, but don't want to live in old-stock rentals. New-stock rentals are the perfect buildings because of the high-quality interiors and modern design they expect.

Retired Couples

Happily retired couples want comfort, a sense of balance in life, and value the fact that everything is included for them—they're going to be taken care of.

We can't stress enough the importance of understanding these different renters so that we can tailor our individual leasing pitches to each and every one of them.

Beyond Those Groups

The feasibility study will have identified the target resident profile. Now is the time to take this a step further and include demographics, psychographics, and household characteristics. This gives us a more in-depth understanding of who these individuals are, how they think, where they live, what they like, and allows us to better tailor our marketing approach.

More importantly, using our grid marketing system, we can then individually target these households on a neighbor-hood-by-neighborhood scale, thus enabling us to not only target all the households likely to become residents, but in addition, target all the neighborhoods that we're likely to attract renters from.

Branding

The first stage after having completed the feasibility study and determining renter profiles is defining the branding. This means getting all the relevant parties together into a design charette. The parties include the architects, interior designers, management lease-up team, general contractor, developers, ad agency, and other consultants. Everyone can then discuss the site, its goals, and provide input and ideas so the brand can be refined into a comprehensive marketing plan.

The People Who Need to Be Hired

Everything comes down to the leasing person. These are the people who are going to determine the value of a building.

Leasing Staff

Once a developer has a great building to lease and the right marketing in place, meeting the customer is where direct interaction occurs. It's here that the competence of the leasing agent comes into play.

A leasing team is likely very small—a maximum of four well-dressed and professional individuals—with strong internet and computer skills and an understanding of the mechanics of doing the job with ease. They also need to be contextually competent and must relate easily to anyone that walks in. Based on the different circumstances encountered, an agent must think on their feet and remain unfazed no matter the situation.

It's also important to give them time to familiarize themselves with the competition and bring them as much material as possible so that they can, in effect, become a pseudo potential renter scouting for a place to live. They'll do a far better job knowing how to position a building in the face of that competition.

The Property Manager

Select a property manager who has prior lease-up experience and a proven track record. A developer needs more than someone looking for management income; they need someone who's motivated to drive revenue. A good way to find out how they work is to visit other sites they've managed and check the level of cleanliness and maintenance. Look for all the little things that separate a so-so building from an extraordinary one. These things make a big difference and help drive the rent.

Communication

Having open communication between the different parties managing the property is vital. To present a consistent, luxurious, and competent message to potential and existing tenants, it's important that at all times everyone is on the same page. This takes constant communication, from those on the front line to those who do the background maintenance.

In the first year, a developer needs a cutting-edge team. After that, a reduced team is enough for maintenance and leasing management. Finding these individuals early is key, as they are the face of the building, and as such, need to be able to convey an owner's values effectively.

Generating Traffic— the Whole Point of Marketing

To generate traffic, nothing beats the internet. Internet leads represent more than half of the traffic that comes across to leasing agents. Smart developers bring on a marketing group that has the skills to design the company web pages, search engine optimization (SEO) and keep the company/developer relevant on social media.

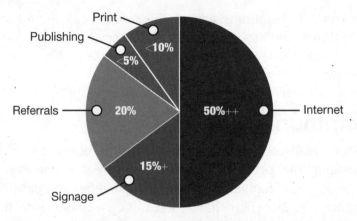

Figure 9.1 - Traffic Generation by Media Source

Although the internet dwarfs all other traffic generators, signage and referrals have not lost their value. A significant amount of continued traffic comes from those marketing vehicles.

Traffic by Unit Type

With different unit types to lease, track how each generates traffic. The goal is to get the same proportion of traffic as the percentage of different units available. There is a way to be predictive like this by tracking the data. This is why we keep talking about tracking traffic—it's vital.

Revenue Management and Pricing Strategies

While doing everything to bring in traffic, is the developer raising rents properly?

A dynamic pricing system adjusts the rents in accordance with the need.

The leasing agent gets compensated for their efforts in driving the rents, and the property manager gets rewarded for making sure everyone is doing their jobs as they should. This is ideal for the merchant apartment builder. They only have one shot at getting this right before the property is sold.

Features and Benefits

A feature is something in the apartment that can be touched—like a temperature control. If there's an extra one in the bedroom, there are benefits to the renters that can be pointed out—such as easily dropping the temperature at night.

The conversion of features to benefits is what makes the sales pitch work. If the building has a gym, the benefits are obvious. For those who find it difficult to go to a gym, having one in the building that's clean and tidy all the time is wonderful—especially in winter. The benefit is that the renter doesn't have to get dressed to go out into the cold if the urge to exercise arises. Pet features will generate a lot of attention. Forty percent of individuals aged 25 own a pet. The benefit in this case is convenience—and those features help keep the building clean.

Offering additional amenities and including them within the marketing material will definitely act as a strong motivator for many renters.

The Benefits of a Written Marketing Plan

A developer should create a system that allows them to maintain and repeat this leasing trajectory. This is done with a written plan. If they're contemplating becoming a merchant apartment builder, having a written system—a handbook—is the key to continued competence.

Once a developer has figured out what the key performance indicators are—from the reams of collected data—they'll be able to stay on top of every situation as they develop.

Conclusion

The value of astute marketing cannot be overstated. It's the key to unlocking both a property's value and wealth generation.

 Marketing is where the money gets made.

With a highly favorable financial environment surrounding the development of rental apartments, a developer owes it to themselves and their financial partners to invest the necessary time and money to develop a comprehensive marketing plan. Once a developer understands renter needs, how to tailor a building's features to match those needs, and their own leasing personalities as it pertains to goals and risk tolerances, a marketing plan can be put into action to maximize achievable rents.

We know that not every developer has the skills and resources to put such a detailed plan into action. However, *we* do.

Oakville—The Taunton Apartments: A Sales Story

Challenge

Experienced developers, Steven Stipsits of Branthaven Homes and Dr. Michael Shih, of Emshih Developments, wanted to enter the apartment development space.

Some 15 years earlier, Dr. Shih had come to Chicago with us on one of our developer trips. We have stayed in touch since. Dr. Shih then introduced us to Steven Stipsits, his partner, a master homebuilder and condo developer. Together, they retained us for a feasibility study for a 284-unit building in Oakville, Ontario. This is an example of developers with a strong vision—one of the things that makes them great individuals. The challenge at hand was that in those individuals, we had two extraordinarily experienced developers who had never built a purpose-built rental apartment before.

The most frequent question they asked was, did the Oakville market have the demand needed to support their vision?

Oakville is one of the richest towns in Canada but had not seen a new apartment built since the 1970s. In our view, demand was extreme—but the developers weren't sure. Our job was to convince them that the demand was actually there. For experienced apartment developers, this would have been easy. But they were new to this business, and very apprehensive.

Action

We completed our feasibility study. Then, over a series of meetings, we attempted to transfer the enthusiasm and confidence we had in that product to the developers, their architect, interior designers, development staff, and their marketing group.

But they were experienced in condo development. They had to be convinced that bigger units would work better than the smaller units that condo developers prefer. The solution was to fly them to the US so we could show them what that apartment market, and their future, looked like.

Very quickly, they understood how that market functioned and what was missing in Oakville.

Result

Condo ≠ Apartment

The people they worked with were smart condo developers who had to shift their way of thinking to build an apartment. They did not have a property management division, so we interviewed the best-in-class property managers. They selected Greenwin. We worked closely with Greenwin to do the lease-up.

That required a great deal of cooperation between the property manager and an outside entity—us. Normally, Greenwin would have leased the building themselves. We went to the developers and made the case that we should handle lease-up and Greenwin should manage. We worked out a cooperative process with Greenwin and the developers. So, instead of two parties during lease-up, there were three.

As a result, we got the highest rents ever achieved in Halton Region. The building was the best designed building in Halton because the developers took the time and spent the money in the appropriate areas to differentiate between a condo and an apartment building.

Testimonial: Michael Shih, Emshih Developments Inc.

Our company was part of the development team that built The Taunton. I first met Derek 20 years ago and followed his new apartment construction program. After attending his seminars and building tours, we engaged him to do a feasibility study, assist with lease-up, and execute final disposition.

We've experienced his Apartment Development FULL Service Experience™ with success, and we continue to use his services.

Street View

Rooftop patio

Figure 9.2 - Oakville - The Taunton Apartments

The Sales and Leasing Plan

Introduction

After two years of full-out effort during the development cycle, a developer shouldn't suddenly relax at the leasing stage.

The lease-up period is when you make all your money.

A successful lease-up period ensures that the crucial investment objectives are achieved. With market-leading rents, the developer stands to make the most money achievable upon stabilization. Therefore, it's imperative that the time used to lease-up an apartment building be used wisely.

Leasing apartments is something we've done for years. This is something we know inside out. Our experience and processes will guide developers through these key components: hiring, training, managing, compensating their frontline leasing staff, and finally, closing the deal. To hit the ground running, they must prepare at least 12 months prior to this critical period and understand the trends and strategies needed for successful lease-up.

However, this is only half of the leasing process; the other half is marketing and operating the building. For more information on marketing, please read book nine, *Writing and Executing the Marketing Plan*, of the *Apartment Development University* series.

Preparation

In preparation for lease-up, there are a few things developers must do, otherwise the rents set might not be achievable.

Unit Preparation

Be Hotel Ready

In apartments, as with hotels, first impressions are key. They color a prospect's entire opinion of a property. By ensuring the lobby is clean and well maintained, and unit interiors are spotless, they can ensure prospects see the property in a positive light.

Model Furniture

The right model furniture makes a unit look welcoming and livable. However, it may create a situation where the model furniture is beyond the means of the renter—to us, that's acceptable. This gives the impression of the space's potential. High-end furniture allows renters to feel a sense of luxury. If they move in, they may very well be able to achieve a similar level of refinement.

Don't Be Chintzy with the Small Stuff

If we recommend a cappuccino machine, then install a good one. We may believe that this particular resident profile is going to value that small touch. We also like to serve appetizing snacks. Small touches like this help make the building stand out from the competition. When trying to lease a $30-million building, put a little extra flair into it.

A Prepared Staff

A way to monitor the leasing staff's performance is to mystery-shop them by phone, email, and in person. What we're looking for is not the things done wrong, but the things done right. If the leasing staff underperforms, it's often because they've been inadequately trained—which is the developer's responsibility. Don't be afraid to add training time if they need it. However, if they underperform consistently and they have been well trained, consider a different course of action. The important point is that mystery shopping is not a negative, but a way to figure out how the leasing staff is performing. Any feedback can be used to modify training and processes as well.

Being a leasing agent is a paid job—salary plus commission. If they can be more effective, their pay will reflect those sales increases. From our experience, great leasing agents want to be adequately trained, and in general, don't mind being monitored.

The Closing Ratio

Marketing shortcomings and underperforming leasing staff adversely affect the closing ratio. Assuming the apartments are in great shape and the leasing staff is stellar, the closing ratio can confirm that rents are set correctly.

We think a 20 percent closing percentage is standard, indicating rents are set very well.

In smaller buildings, that 20 percent is less meaningful. A small number of closings will affect that percentage greatly. However, in a larger building (200 units or more), a larger number of potential renters must be seen in order to meet the developer's goals. If lease-up drags on, seasonal leasing patterns may also come into play. Not closing 20 percent might indicate a marketing problem as well—the right prospects aren't being attracted to the building. And if they are, the leasing staff might be underperforming. However, if the leasing staff is closing well, but are leasing only one type of unit, this indicates pricing is an issue—something that needs to be quickly addressed.

We expect a very high level of competence from our leasing teams, from leasing feedback and regular reports, to high situational awareness. When issues arise, we expect the team to respond quickly, keeping closing ratios high and rents set as high as achievable.

Leasing for Maximum Rents

What should an apartment leasing look like and how does a developer train their leasing team to achieve it?

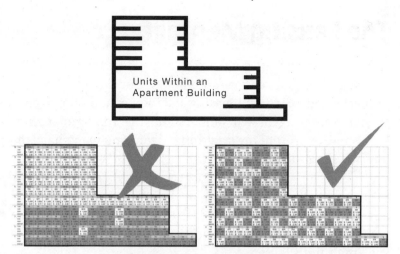

Figure 10.1 - Leasing Patterns

The orange boxes are the leased-out units, and the white boxes are not yet leased. The left-hand graphic shows what happens when leasing is not carefully monitored and controlled. Leasing units should result in a random checkerboard pattern across unit types and unit price. The leasing agents should carefully watch the units that get the most traffic and interest, and act quickly and nimbly to increase the price on these. This has the effect of moving prospective residents into other unit types to ensure that no single stack leases up too quickly.

For example, if the view premiums are priced too high, renters will simply accept a lower floor (see the left-hand side of the graphic). Don't be left in a situation where all the lower floors are rented, thus forcing a drop in upper-floor rents just to get them occupied. The goal is to have a mix of units available throughout the lease-up period and not quickly run out of any unit types or price.

Once the building is stabilized, renting becomes much less complicated. That's not to say staff can switch to autopilot, but they can establish a rhythm of leasing out units as they turn over and collect the best possible rents.

The Leasing Mentality

Apartment sales staff have a relatively short time to "sell" a unit to a potential renter—only hours. Our advice is to stick to specialized apartment-leasing staff, not condo sales agents. A good rental agent will understand the renter mentality, know how to present the sizzle effectively, and won't have the internal biases that may affect sales.

With up to 30 percent turnover every year, a building is effectively entirely re-rented every three to four years. As an owner, the developer is dependent on that sizzle to be able to keep their units leased.

The Importance of Training

The leasing agent is the closest person to the customer. They know the value proposition and they know why people rent in the building. Their market knowledge can help a developer raise rents surgically. During lease-up, please ask the leasing agents for any insights they may have. They can provide valuable feedback.

We think the training of leasing staff is important for three reasons.

Why is Lease-up Training So Important?

1. **Attracting new residents through:**
   - Marketing
   - Good salesmanship
2. **Keeping existing residents through:**
   - Customer service
   - Proactive lease renewal
3. **Professionally raising rents**

Figure 10.2 - Training is Key

After attracting new residents through marketing and good salesmanship, leasing agents ensure rental stability by providing good customer service and proactive lease renewal. The person who does the leasing almost becomes the customer service manager for that renter. This may cause problems down the road when the developer needs leasing staff to focus on leasing—property management should be taking care of customer service. But at times, renters do return to the rental office staff because they've developed a friendly relationship.

The retention plan should start on the day that people first move in. A great move-in experience will mean that the renter will stay and not think about moving out. Potentially, rents must rise as time goes on. Therefore, the owner needs them to appreciate the value of the building. If the market moves up or there's some rent left on the table, they may be able to make up the difference in the second year. However, doing that is much harder to do.

The whole idea is to get rents right the first time.

Typical Renter Objections

What really happens on leasing sites? What are the common exchanges between leasing agent and potential renter? We're assuming it's a great, and clean, building, the apartments are ready, the models attractive, and everything else is ready for rental. When a prospect is asked if they would like to lease a unit, they typically respond in one of four ways:
- I need to think about it
- I need to check it out with my spouse/partner/ roommate
- It's too much money
- This is the first apartment I've seen

Since we know what the common objections are, preparing for them in advance ensures these objections don't derail the leasing process.

Motivation

While training, it's wise to put into place a system of motivation and compensation that fits the company's structure and culture. Not everyone wants to be compensated in the same way. They've got a history of how they've done things. There are many different ways to compensate people.

The Leasing Agent Rules

Training is not an event, it's a process. We've been training leasing staff in the apartment industry for decades. After initial training, we know it should be refreshed to prevent slipping back into old habits. That way, agents stay on top of their game.

Let the professional leasing agent do their work. If a developer expects top-of-the-market prices—hire agents who know how to achieve that. Leasing is top dog during lease-up time—that's where a developer's priority should be. This means not expecting them to cold-call or hand out flyers when their primary focus should be on the actual leasing and follow up with prospects. Let the professionals work within their realm of expertise.

The Perfect Resident

The objective is to find the perfect resident: one who will enjoy the building's features, continue to live in the community, and renew their lease for another year.

Referrals are a great source of leads, often around 20 percent—sometimes higher. Those referrals, in reality, have already been sold on the building. The staff's responsibility is to confirm what they already know about the building and close the deal. The closing ratio for referrals is typically much higher (as high as 80 percent). These prospects have been pre-qualified because they know the rents and the community, and they actively want to reside there.

Leasing Cycles and Variable Terms

All leases come up for renewal at some point. Looking forward to that time; it's wise to renew when re-leasing is easiest. This means that leases shouldn't't be fixed at 12 months—the term should be variable.

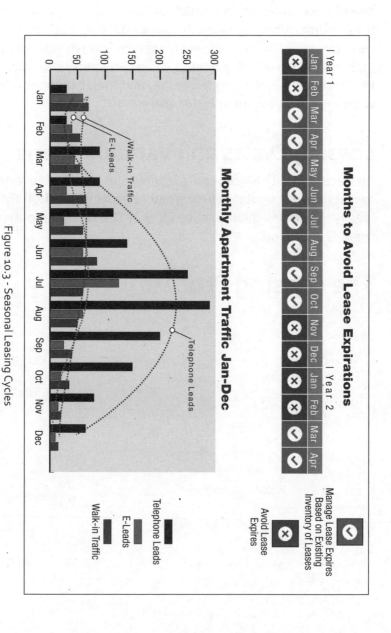

Figure 10-3 - Seasonal Leasing Cycles

It's clear from the graph in Figure 10.3 that leasing is a seasonal business. Leases coming due in colder months— November to February—are more difficult to re-lease because traffic is very low. If initial lease-up happens to occur during those months and there's been success due to marketing prowess, variable term leases make sense. For leases coming due in the winter months, we recommend a 16-month lease, so renewal is in April—peak-leasing season.

However, don't get into a situation where a large percentage of leases expire at the same time, even if it's during peak-leasing season. If many renters decide to move, the leasing agent is stuck refilling a large number of units over a very short time. Spread out the lease expiry dates to prevent that.

The Leasing Process

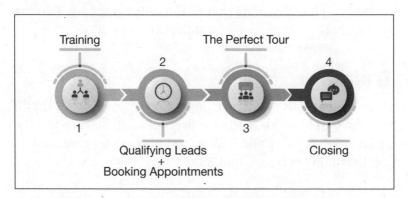

Figure 10.4 - The Leasing Process

Though it may seem like a simple four-step process, the details are extremely important when taking the process from one that's adequate to one that surpasses expectations.

To lease a building, look for people who are smart and can think on their feet. Remember, they're not selling widgets; they're making very specific sales to very specific people. Knowing their product and knowing their renter means they can sell to all those who qualify—from young professionals to senior couples—with equal ease and aplomb. Those different individuals should be shown the features that matter to the renter at hand, stress the unit advantages that make sense, but still stay focused on the basic principles of making a successful deal.

Track the Marketing Dollars

There is likely going to be a lot of money spent at this early stage. Monitor all traffic so it is clear how effective the dollars are. Everything can be logged, and with technology, traffic can be monitored in detail: telephone, internet, signage, social media, etc. All of this can be compiled into detailed reports to help make decisions. With good traffic data, further refine the marketing plan: put more money into things that are working well and take money away from those that aren't.

Training

Have leasing staff shop the competition. Paid to do so, they'll take time before the leasing office opens to learn what the competition is doing and how to best prepare for renters who will inevitably compare buildings.

Shopping the competition gives the leasing team a competitive edge and confidence to elevate their building so it becomes the market leader. A well-prepared leasing agent will make a world of difference to the bottom line. If the goal is to be best in class, having agents see what subpar leasing looks like helps them rise above that standard. In this way, the potential renter is impressed instead of experiencing the same old service they expected.

Qualifying Leads

The objective is to place all effort into viable opportunities, not waste time with those who won't likely rent, no matter the reason.

Indicate the Rents

Display the rents front and center, essentially pre-qualifying leads, ensuring that they're not only interested in the building, but are also capable of paying the rents charged.

What Does the Renter Want?

What are a potential renter's needs? If the building can accommodate their needs, wonderful. If not, they may choose to search elsewhere.

Talk Up Features

Increase a prospect's interest by talking about the property in terms of features and benefits in a sincere way, using very positive words to expound on the building's benefits. This can include a discussion about appliances, high-efficiency fixtures, easy-to-clean flooring, and amenities, which will help facilitate their lifestyle. Remember that when leasing, show prospects not just the value offered, but also how they can personally benefit by moving in.

Make an Appointment

The primary purpose of the phone call is to make an appointment so that they'll come in and visit. At that time, open a dialogue with an aim to close. Without traffic, no leases get signed and no bonuses get paid.

The Perfect Tour

Though many potential renters want to see the apartment they're interested in before touring the building, the most effective tour begins after they have an understanding of the building's amenities, features, and how these benefit them. This lets the building's advantages sink in before seeing the unit's features, thus making the asked rent reasonable.

Don't waste time showing a person an apartment that fundamentally doesn't suit their needs (functionally or budget-wise). Sit down with a potential renter and have a significant discussion with them before rushing off on the tour. Don't show them an apartment they don't want, one where their furniture won't fit in, doesn't complement their lifestyle, or they can't afford. Take the time to find out who you're renting to and show them what works for them. By preparing the leasing agent with floor plan audits, rent roll expectations, and the features and benefits of the location, building, and unit, they will be able to sell the unit effectively and move to a point where closing is likely.

Closing

The great Canadian hockey player and philosopher Wayne Gretzky said, "You miss 100 percent of the shots you never take."

For whatever reason, there are agents who just don't want to close. It's like they're afraid of the rejection, even though rejection is part of the job. There's no harm done. It simply means they tried their best and can now move on to the next prospect.

Some potential renters will close on the agent before the agent has a chance to close on them. They'll say, "I'll take it," before the presentation is finished. Stop selling and go back to the leasing office to get it done. There will always be a percentage of units that lease quickly with minimal effort. But a great sales team will get a much greater percentage leased, turning what could have been a slow lease-up into a very successful lease-up. In effect, the training they've been given has made the owner a handsome amount of money.

By knowing how to respond to common objections, the leasing agent keeps the dialogue going. Sometimes, time is all they need. Once a renter processes all the information, they'll quickly decide what to do.

Effective Closing Methods

Preparing for these specific closing techniques can give a leasing agent that extra confidence boost when unsure how or when to close. As with all training, this requires practice and repetition in order to be perfect. But as always, if they never bother trying to close, they'll never succeed in doing so.

The "Assumptive" Close

Make the assumption that the prospect is going to rent. If the tour went well and the prospects are enthused and planning their lives in the unit, assume they will close.

The "Double OK" Close

"You can enjoy this unit very soon, all I need is your OK. OK?" With this kind of assurance, an agent has leased an apartment and can begin the paperwork. All they needed to do was to give the prospect permission to say "OK."

The "I Want to Think It Over" Close

To prevent or restart a stalled dialogue, a leasing agent may want to encourage the prospect to reveal the actual stumbling block. "Is it the price?" Even though the agent moved to pricing quickly, they felt they had a good enough rapport to do so. Making the prospect aware of what they're gaining by living here helps bridge the monetary gap.

The "No" Close

"Do you have any questions before we begin the paperwork?"

"No."

Assuming the leasing agent has done their homework and carefully listened to the prospect, they'll know how serious the objection is and how to counter it effectively so a close can happen.

In Summation

Most closes can be done by experienced leasing agents pretty naturally. The fear of asking for a close should be set aside— even left at home.

Agents also don't want to be pushy—developers don't want that either. It doesn't work. But by building a rapport with the prospects, reading them accurately, and having a premium product to sell, a leasing agent has earned the right to ask if the potential renter wants to lease. Most prospects will not be offended. They know that the question of leasing must come up at some point. The leasing agent's job is to know when that is and just do it.

Trust the Process

Why aren't sales agents closing—is it fear of rejection? Remember, the prospect is saying no to the opportunity, not to the agent. It's not personal. It's something beyond an agent's control: price, location, or distance from work.

Figure 10.5 - Do Not FEAR

Above all, an agent should believe in the product and trust both their training and the process.

Conclusion

"The leasing agent, during initial lease-up, determines the building's value."
– Derek Lobo

With the right training, adequate research at their disposal, and supported by great marketing, the leasing team will make the developer and investor happy.

"What gets measured, gets done. What gets measured and paid for, gets done better."
– Tom Peters

To keep agents motivated, compensate them well for their efforts. Compensation does need to be paid based on the developer's company's culture. And put in place a bonus structure.

Pay agents a reasonable base rate because they don't know how much they're going to make. Then add individual bonuses and team bonuses once they reach a certain level so there's a sense of the group working together.

Listen to the leasing team closely and do what's needed to support them. The leasing agent's role in lease-up is crucial. A developer must do everything they can to make their leasing staff work as seamlessly and uneventfully as possible, giving them the necessary tools and room to focus so they can fulfill their roles as leasing professionals.

Always remember, rent determines a building's value, so it's worthy of a developer's full attention!

Barrie—Ferndale Gardens: A Sales Story

Challenge

Prior to this project, we had met Eli Turk of Pinemount Developments and worked with him in various capacities. Pinemount Developments is a second-generation real estate company with holdings in many asset classes. Their first major apartment project was 430 Ferndale.

Turk had bought a piece of land and then went to the city to increase the density, creating real value for the project. I was impressed with the amount of research they had done and the time they took to get the first building right. I find that if a developer doesn't execute optimally the first time, it impacts what could be a significant development pipeline. It's important to get the first project done properly and make a good profit to set a precedent, thus setting a good foundation for their future development business.

We stayed in touch with them throughout the development process, touring the property and updating market comparables. The building's design and amenity space fit well with the demographic they targeted.

Unfortunately, they hired a third-party manager with little new-apartment experience. Leasing got off to a slow start, with the renters cherry-picking the smallest units. So, instead of leasing like a checkerboard, they had mostly leased the small units. Please refer to *Writing and Executing a Sales and Leasing Plan*, book 10 in the *Apartment Development University* series for more information about sales and leasing plans.

Part way through the process we were called in to take over the leasing process.

Action

We immediately reset the rents upward, though it was in a difficult leasing environment, and stepped up the sales and marketing profiles. Given the seriousness of the situation and the developer's desire to sell, we moved one of our trained rental agents into the building and they leased continuously.

It's not typical to move an agent into a building, but when there is an emergency situation, every effort has to be made, and this was a good way to get things back on track.

To boost walk-in traffic, we decided to supplement our online marketing efforts with some old-fashioned tactics—outdoor signage. The property sat on one of Barrie, Ontario's, major arteries. By adding A-frame signage on the street with balloons, it sent a message to anyone driving by that our leasing office was open and to please come in. It was simple but effective.

Because our agent was in the building at all times, opening hours became unimportant, allowing prospects to just show up and be well served.

Result

When we reached about 70 percent occupancy, we brought in an offer from an institutional buyer who went firm. We continued leasing very successfully. At closing, the building was 90 percent occupied.

Testimonial: Eli Turk, Pinemount Developments Ltd.

We have built a long-term relationship with Derek and his team, relying on them on our project at 430 Ferndale, and other projects, for rent setting, joint venture structuring, brokerage, and marketing.

Their company provides complete services for apartment developers; this was particularly useful to us in our business. The apartment data and insights that Derek and his team provided us, helped us make better-informed and intelligent decisions.

We value their results-driven consulting abilities.

Street view

Figure 10.6 - Barrie - Ferndale Gardens

The Four Factors That Drive Rent

Introduction

While rent has the biggest impact on a development's profitability, it's also the most difficult to nail down. A developer knows what their land costs are, what their construction costs are going to be, and that they can make educated guesses as to their taxes and utility costs. However, they can't guess what the cap rate and rents will be—the market determines that.

The four factors that determine what a developer can charge for rent are:
1. Location
2. Unit design and size
3. Amenities
4. Property management

Why Rent Matters

So, why does rent matter that much?

To help answer that question, take a close look at this formula:

**NET OPERATING INCOME / CAPITALIZATION RATE
= PURCHASE PRICE**

For example:

**$100 IN RENT X 12 (MONTHS) / 5% CAPITALIZATION RATE
= $24,000 IN VALUE**

What this says is for the building described in the Development Scenario graphic below (Figure 11.1), if rent is increased by $100 over a 12-month period at a 5 percent capitalization, it equates to $24,000 in increased value—for a single unit. When multiplied out across an entire building, this minor increase in rent has a substantial effect on the property's overall value.

Building Size
- 270 units
- 220,000 net rentable SQFT

Market
- Urban, High-rise

Return on Cost
- 29% margin

Assumptions
- Rent = $2.80
- Operating Costs ~26%

Figure 11.1 - Development Scenario

If we raise rents by 5 percent and reduce operating expenses and hard costs by 5 percent as follows:

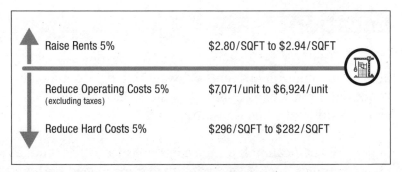

Raise Rents 5%	$2.80/SQFT to $2.94/SQFT
Reduce Operating Costs 5% (excluding taxes)	$7,071/unit to $6,924/unit
Reduce Hard Costs 5%	$296/SQFT to $282/SQFT

Figure 11.2 - Sensitivity Analysis

These are the results:

Base Profit	$32 million
Raise Rent 5%	**$8 million extra value**
Reduce Operating Costs 5%	$1 million extra value
Reduce Hard Costs 5%	$3.5 million extra value

Figure 11.3 - Case Results

Raising rents by 5 percent equates to an increase of approximately $0.14 per square foot. Though a relatively small amount, when reflected in the impact on the ultimate valuation, this 5 percent increase can add an additional $8 million to the bottom line. That's a much greater increase than the 5 percent reduction in operating expenses and hard costs gives, both of which are very difficult to accomplish.

It's clear that getting the right rents from the very beginning, especially for a developer intending to sell a property, is vital.

Location

The old real estate maxim, "Location, location, location," applies to rental apartments as well as single homes and condos. If a building is not built in the right location, it's not going to attract the highest rents.

Superiority of location is a subjective measure. It's dependent on many things, such as accessibility to transit, neighborhood character, and proximity to community amenities. But once a superior location is found, it attracts renters willing to pay higher rents. Alternatively, inferior locations have the opposite effect and often rely on lower rents to fully lease-up.

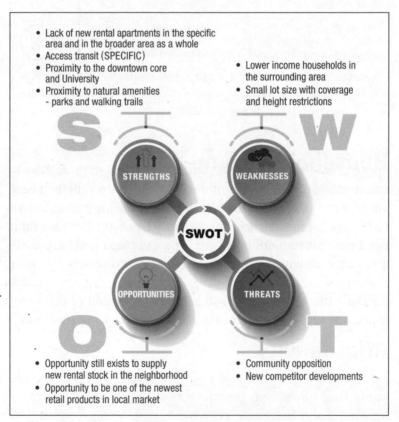

Figure 11.4 - SWOT Analysis

SWOT Analysis

In the quest to understand what makes a good rental location (as it pertains to purpose-built rental) we consider four aspects of any site: its Strengths, its Weaknesses, the Opportunities, and the Threats.

To figure out how to set base rents, we study household income, affordability, average rents, comparable buildings (new and old stock rentals), and condo comparables.

1. Setting Base Rents

In a new rental product, we need to attract new renters, many of which will be downsizing. These potential renters are currently homeowners. There's no point limiting the opportunity to only attracting current renters—they shouldn't be the target. The goal is to expand the developer's reach to those who now own their homes.

Household Income

The analysis of median household incomes in specific areas allows us to see how much rent can reasonably be charged. If the proposed building needs rents beyond what potential renters can afford, it's not feasible to build. Be cognizant of the fact that students and downsizers may have lower incomes but higher abilities to rent due to parental support for the former and significant investments for the latter.

Affordability

Who lives in the area and how much can they afford? We know that affordable rent is about 30 percent of monthly income. From there, we take what people can theoretically afford and subtract CMHC's average rent. This becomes the difference between what people can actually pay and what the current market is performing at.

Average Rents

Data usually shows what current stock is achieving now, not in the future. However, it does give a baseline of what is achievable in the marketplace based on the type of currently available product.

Comparables

When setting rents, study the strengths of a specific location relative to comparable locations. Potential renters do notice the difference between parquet, older carpeting, and new laminate flooring. In-suite laundry is a huge plus. The level of finish, the attention to small things like light fixtures, and how well the units are designed, does not go unnoticed.

Setting Rents

Potential renters will compare one building to another and make decisions quickly. In their minds, how a building ranks in value determines where they will decide to move. Once that is understood, a developer can determine where their building fits in. Is it better overall? Is it worse or comparable? Then they can evaluate each of their units to each of the comparables' units.

Although this sounds like a great deal of effort, rent setting is equal parts science and intuition. Have full awareness of local comparables and demographics in the form of collected data, and also, an awareness of the neighborhood's specific attributes likely to affect a building's attractiveness. Every extra dollar charged keeps coming month after month, year after year—it quickly adds up. Therefore, make the effort, get into the numbers and all the pluses and minuses—it will make a huge difference.

2. Unit Size and Design

Depending on the market and target resident profile, units will either be viewed, more-or-less favorably, by residents. Higher favorability typically means a unit will be able to attract more prospective tenants, who will in turn be willing to pay a premium for the privilege of living in a well-appointed and nicely designed unit. It's up to the developer to find out what works in a particular location so that they design rental units to best suit potential renters.

Unit Size

The following graph illustrates how rent compares to unit size. As you can see, the two are not directly related for all sizes.

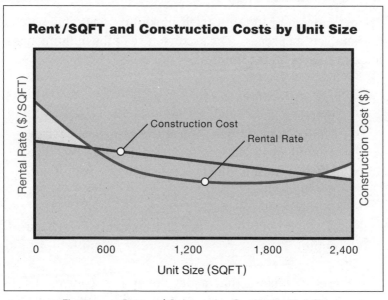

Figure 11.5 - Rent and Construction Cost Versus Unit Size

A smaller unit does not necessarily have to rent at a lower rate. Larger units do not always achieve higher rents, but they sometimes do, as in the case of premium units. The result: if rents are set solely based on square footage, the maximum rents may not be achieved. The beginning and end of the graph indicates that it's more nuanced than that. Also, don't think about rent-roll in terms of setting just one rent per unit type.

Floor Plan Audit

Price each unit based individually on their layout, features, and finishes. Those with the greatest functionality achieve the highest rents. By combining the traditional square footage and bedroom count with functionality, a developer can price units in a way potential renters can easily see the value inherent in those prices.

External Factors

Factors outside of the unit itself make up a valuable part of the rent-setting process. The architecture of the building has a huge influence on the unit's desirability.

Consider these factors:
- View
- The balcony/outdoor space (private, large, wrap-around, open air)
- Floor (ground floor, lower floor, top floor, penthouse)
- Distance to elevators
- Noise potential (elevator shaft, stairwell, garbage chute)

These are all factors that a developer can control before construction begins—at the design stage. These must be considered carefully as they directly impact the rent each unit can achieve.

Internal Factors

Once a renter steps inside the unit, another set of rent-setting factors come into play.
These factors include:

- Functionality of the layout
- Storage
- Kitchen layout and features
- Bathroom access
- Dens (size, storage, potential bedroom)
- Potential entertainment wall

Prospective renters do notice these factors and take them into account. A well-designed and functional unit will pay great rents month after month.

3. Amenities

Along with unit design, amenities are an important factor in attracting tenants. The right amenity package can ensure a building's continued competitiveness in any given market long after the building's completion. Amenities not only act as rent drivers, but also, as additional utility for residents, making them feel that they're getting more value for their mental dollar. Note that while condominium buyers see dramatic amenities as a monthly expense over and above what they paid for their unit, renters see them as extra value for their rent.

A condo buyer buys the steak.
A renter buys the sizzle.

A building's beautiful lobby (and wonderful arrival experience) and great amenities are a leasing agent's best tools for getting prospective tenants interested in renting, and generally results in higher rents, higher building valuation, and higher takeout financing. A renter is attracted to what they see—amenities are a major part of that. However, a condo buyer is literally just buying the physical structure.

The overarching theme is that with strong amenitization, a developer no longer needs to compete on rent alone, because those amenities, along with the features and finishes, help sell the rent as having plenty of value.

Amenities in a Multi-phased Development

For a multi-phase site, or in a site that contains both old and new buildings, providing a separate clubhouse is an excellent way to reduce amenity requirements in the gross leasable area (GLA), but add to the renter's experience. A smart developer will be able to increase overall density because the amenity space is no longer eating into the leasable area. It provides a centrally located amenity space with minimal interference and maximum benefits to all the buildings.

Luxury Products

Luxury or ultra-luxury rentals in a suburban location need a very high level of amenitization—higher than comparable condo buildings. But when building in an urban location, the developer only wants to provide as many amenities as they think are reasonably appropriate.

Ultra-luxury buildings offer entire floors dedicated to amenities. When charging $4,000 for a one-bedroom plus den, it is important to convince renters not just that the finishes and features are appropriate, but that the building will benefit their lifestyle. These amenities include movie theaters, game rooms, co-working spaces, meeting spaces, lounge areas, and indoor or outdoor pools. The aim is to provide the maximum benefit to residents.

The Need for Amenitization

A developer is likely to succeed during lease-up if they offer a strong amenity package. But that amenity space competes with their net leasable area. They need to be cognizant of the actual requirements. In a market with limited competition, or in a suburban location, a developer should always include fewer amenities.

However, a developer shouldn't provide more amenity space than they're comfortable with. It's a balancing act. The first priority is maximizing the number of units. But at the same time, if the developer doesn't provide enough amenity space, it will reduce a building's attractiveness long term, forcing them to compete on rents. With strong amenitization, they don't have to.

4. Property Management

The fourth factor affecting rent, one that many developers don't adequately understand, is a building's property management platform. This refers to the leasing agent (usually a team) in charge of renting the apartments. A building's rent is set to a large extent by how well the building's leasing and marketing teams sell and market the building.

Conclusion

Rent has the biggest impact on pro forma—nothing else comes close.

The four factors affecting rent are all in the developer's control.

We have years of experience, a large portion of which is focused on honing these four with only one goal—maximizing the achievable rent for each and every unit. Developers are strongly encouraged to take advantage of that experience so that they may reap the rewards associated with building an apartment that not only pays for itself, but also, generates years of income.

Thornhill—Foresite Suites: A Sales Story

Challenge

Buy-side brokerage is a vehicle to create more transactions: find a qualified buyer and have that buyer pay the broker and transact the building. In this case, the broker works for the buyer, not the seller.

Entrepreneur Alan Greenberg was searching to find a suitable boutique apartment building to buy, with the intention to convert it to a suite hotel. Alan retained us to find a suitable investment property for conversion. By chance, I came across such a property—we thought it was the perfect building.

Action

The conversion of a conventional apartment building to a suite hotel is, in a sense, a non-economic sale. The buyer doesn't want the building for its intended purpose, hence, that buyer is more concerned with how much the building will be ultimately worth.

The buyer was looking at it through different eyes—looking at the business through the eyes of a hotel owner. This was a new experience for me. It was an interesting education for us to think about conversion to a different use.

Result

Alan Greenberg now put together a group of investors.

Developer Neil Zaret, and his son Josh Zaret, became the managing partners for Foresite Suites. They successfully converted the building to a furnished suite operation that they operated for many years. Over that time, we developed a relationship with the Zarets so when it came time to sell the building, we were given the opportunity to bring an institutional buyer to the table, and then, transacted.

We sold to KingSett Capital.

However, after several years of ownership, KingSett decided it was time to sell and focus on larger buildings. They were very kind to come back to us to sell the building; they called it a "full ride" and listed with us.

Testimonial: Neil Zaret, Gemstone Developments

I met Derek in 2007 as part of a group that he introduced to a building. With his help, we completed the purchase and successfully managed a combined apartment and furnished suite building.

Since that time, Derek and I have stayed in touch. When the group decided to sell that building, it made perfect sense to utilize him for the sale. Again, we negotiated a successful transaction. Derek and his team are a pleasure to work with.

Street view

Figure 11.6 - Thornhill - Foresite Suites

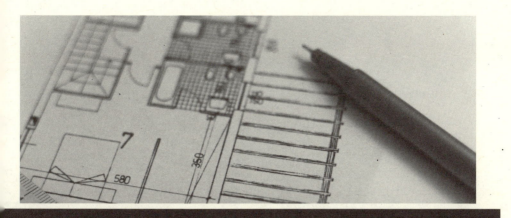

PART 5: Selling
Your Apartment

The Merchant Builder

Introduction

The more clearly a developer can answer the question, "Are you building to keep or are you building to sell?" the straighter and cleaner the path will be to achieving the intended goals. Though many developers intend to keep a building, if the opportunity arises to sell at a handsome profit, they may do so. Once they see how much can be made selling a building, they may decide to programmatically build to sell, holding on to only a very few properties for the ongoing income. Note, that when we refer to "programmatic," we mean using a specific process or methodology to cover all the specialized steps involved.

> *"There's a fixed supply of apartments in Canada, and more and more people are chasing that fixed supply. Buying apartments through the traditional broker route will become more and more expensive as time goes on .Apartments are the way forward."*
>
> *– John Love, CEO, KingSett Capital*

We think John Love is right. The demand for apartments is even higher now than it was before the COVID-19 pandemic.

One of the ways to look at life is saying, "I'm going to make the pie bigger," instead of, "I'm going to go after the same pie and try and buy." Expanding the pie is always a better strategy. Creating a product that everybody wants to buy is a far better strategy than buying a product that everybody is competing for. There's an unlimited amount of business share for the merchant apartment builder.

Even though a developer has the skills to build, it doesn't mean they have the skills to develop a successful business. In the same way that the person sourcing funds to build a project needs different skills from the person who constructs the building, developing a sound business plan is yet another important skill. To become a programmatic builder, continually building rental apartments, maintaining a steady cash flow, and having the ability to fund future projects, developers must look beyond the projects they're currently working on to those that will grow the business over an extended period. They must learn to manage project opportunities and decide how the wealth they're creating will be best used, managed, and handed down to future generations.

The apartment builder from the 60s and 70s was probably the most successful real estate developer in North America. Nobody remembers the homebuilders of the period, but the apartment buildings of that time are still here, and still generating income for those developers' children and grandchildren. Even if the developer sold their building, some other party is reaping the benefits decades later. It's all about wealth preservation, tax deferral, maintaining cash flow, and ensuring the business prospers and meets the owner's goals.

Apartments require very little management when stabilized. Once a capable third-party asset manager is hired to watch over the buildings, it leaves the developer, their children, and their grandchildren, the freedom to enjoy the benefits of wealth preservation.

Preparing for the Next Generation

The ideals of a merchant builder are more akin to that of a condo developer in that when they finish a project (either sold or kept), they move on to the next, continuously expanding their portfolio (of both buildings kept and buildings sold).

This chapter is less about real estate and more about developing a business plan to become a merchant apartment builder, which means it's really about the developer's business and family. Some families don't want to jeopardize their basic standard of living, and therefore, focus on maintaining what the founder has built. Others want to enhance their lifestyle and take their company to the next level. This means taking on more risk and reinvesting in new apartment construction.

However, many families fail to properly plan for the next generation's handling of their assets. We've asked many owners, "What did the founder, that apartment developer, that great man or woman who had this vision and the courage to take risks, really want?" The answer: they wanted to preserve the value of their assets. And they wanted their children to become productive adults, their grandchildren to be taken care of, and last but not least, they wanted their families to get along once they were gone.

We have spent the last 30+ years working with development families. We know that with the proper planning, moving wealth from generation to generation can be both efficient and practical.

What We Do

As a company, we've spent our lives working with apartment developers and we firmly believe that apartment buildings are the best way for a real estate family to transition wealth from one generation to the next.

It's clear that becoming a successful apartment developer does not have to be an overly complex process that leaves owners confused and discouraged. Over the years, we have built a formula that really works—our clients are testament to that. This formula is available to any asset developer interested in taking as much of the guesswork out of apartment building as possible, relying instead on our proven system that informs every step of development, from project conception to either selling after completion, or holding it for years of steady income.

Our company is well equipped to formulate a working plan that will ensure a stable income for future generations.

The Merchant Builder's Business Plan

The key to succeed as a merchant apartment builder is to develop a business plan. This is done by completing a full review of strengths, intentions, and goals as a developer.

A merchant developer should ask themselves these questions:
- Is the goal to grow a portfolio for future generations (build and hold)?
- Is the goal to build on prior experience and hold a cash reserve (build and sell)?
- What are our strengths as a developer?

Once the intentions and goals are fully understood, business decisions can be made that keep these points in mind.

The Benefits

What are the benefits of becoming a merchant apartment builder compared to the development of other asset classes?

Construction Can Be Halted Quickly

In smaller markets, the developer can build a phased product. If the project is four 50-unit apartments, for a total of 200 units, and something goes wrong in any way, the developer can pivot and take that land, and do something else with it, such as building condos or retail. When building out a project that may go for 14 months, the developer is never more than 14 months away from stopping the business. However, we don't think there are any reasons to do so as apartment buildings are quite recession proof.

Short-Term Leases

Unit leases are relatively short term. That gives an opportunity to react to marketplace conditions, as rents and cost of operations vary year over year. Rents can be adjusted and be reflected within the rent roll relatively quickly.

Single Tenants Occupy Relatively Small Spaces

This is an important one—no single tenant occupies a huge amount of space. For a shopping center operator, a single grocery anchor may occupy 60 percent of the leasable space, with smaller businesses representing relatively small overall proportions of the remaining space. In a rental building, however, with potentially hundreds of individual tenants, when a single tenant leaves, there are many others who continue to pay rent.

Predictable Capital Expenditure

The outlay for capital expenditures is very predictable. With a greater number of tenants, the risk of non-payment becomes spread out and diluted. This means that rental owners are insulated to some extent from the problems affecting renters, resulting in greater flexibility and a more predictable cash flow.

Everyone Needs Shelter

A developer cannot outsource rental. Renting offers flexibility to people, regardless of life stage or situation. This includes both those capable and those unable to afford their own homes. With such a diverse customer profile, providing rental apartments is a relatively recession-proof industry.

The Merchant Builder's Checklist

How does a developer find out what to build and where to build it? The answer is the Opportunity Analysis, covered earlier in this book.

For more on the Opportunity Analysis, see Chapter 1: The Feasibility Study

Figure 12.1 - The Merchant Builders Checklist

Of paramount importance is the first checkmark: is the developer building to hold or sell?

The importance of this question cannot be overstated. It determines the goals for that project, setting the foundation for many of the decisions that follow.

Conclusion

It's abundantly clear that becoming a merchant builder is a winning path for developers wishing to grow their business, and at the same time provide a means of support for their family and successors over future generations.

The means to meet these goals is fully within the reach of any developer who, over the years, takes advantage of the support we give them. With a full understanding of the implications of the answer to "The Big Question" (next chapter), the wealth-generation engine inherent in the apartment business can be fully utilized.

London—Ironstone Townhouses: A Sales Story

 ## Challenge

Allan Drewlo grew up in the apartment business. My first recollection of him was when I did some work for his family— he was still in high school.

Today, Allan has taken over the family business and continues the tradition of building high-quality apartments. His company is an apartment machine. For example, when his company buys kitchens, they buy 1,000 at a time. They usually buy in bulk and don't customize their individual units. Asking him to customize one kitchen, never mind all of them, is frowned upon. When there is such a successful machine, why change and potentially put it at risk? Drewlo would never let anyone alter his winning formula.

However, Drewlo wanted to build his own brand. With long-time business partner Dave Stimac, they formed Ironstone Building Company to build for-sale rental products. Ironstone would build apartments similar to the parent company, but with the intent to sell instead of holding.

Action

Over the years, we had discussed with the partners the building-for-sale concept.

The advice I give all new merchant builders, and to Ironstone at the time, is to build what they're comfortable with when moving into a new asset class. One challenge (going from keeping to selling the buildings) is enough.

Ironstone wisely chose an efficient form they had built many times before, repurposing it as a for-sale rental project. However, they were still apprehensive about the sale of this project. They wanted surety of closing with no hiccups.

Result

In response, we brought in the largest buyer in Canada. Mark Kenney, CAPREIT (Canadian Apartment REIT). The largest REIT in Canada, CAPREIT is known for its no-nonsense business approach. It will value a building at a fair price and close. In this case, it did just that, and Ironstone Housing was pleased with the result.

Testimonial: Mark Kenney, President of CAPREIT

 CAPREIT has purchased over 1,000 units with Derek and his team, and all of the transactions have come from deep relationships with the apartment owner and developer.

Understanding relationships has allowed Derek to grow his brokerage into one of the most active in Canada.

Testimonial: Dave Stimac, Ironstone Building Company

 I'm relatively new to the apartment business, but my partner and Derek are highly experienced. Derek's vast marketing knowledge, coupled with his impressive network of the strongest buyers in the country, helped us successfully close our first apartment transaction.

Thanks to Derek's support throughout the sales process, our first foray into the apartment business went very smoothly. As a result, we anticipate more for-sale apartment projects to supplement our core single-family home and townhome business.

Double garage townhouse

Street view row of townhouses

Figure 12.2 - London - Ironstone Townhouses

The
Big Question

Introduction

The business of apartment buildings always comes back to that one big question: is the developer building to hold or sell? Put another way, how is the developer going to end the project? A developer should not underestimate the importance of making the sell-hold decision as early in the building process as possible, preferably as part of their long-term business model before any single building project has begun.

Figure 13.1 - The Big Question

This has been mentioned time and time again, not only because it's an important consideration, but because the decision made can also change with time. Not every developer who builds to hold ends up holding on to their properties forever, especially once they've recognized the value in their developments and the potential proceeds from a sale.

Why This Decision Is Vital

The hold or sell discussion is about long-term goals and family. It's about a developer's ongoing business model combined with their longer-term goals—including those of the generations that follow. Often with first-time developers, the long view into the future is not fully formed. The current project consumes them; the goal is simply to make as much money as possible. But a few projects in, the long-term goals become clearer as the need to direct the proceeds from a past project as efficiently and cost-effectively as possible becomes more pressing.

To make this possible, we have developed an exclusive process based on our unique experience, knowledge, and skills to best serve developer families in these situations. Please refer to the next chapter, "Intergenerational Wealth," for more information.

Liquidity Concerns

If the developer intends to sell a new building, they need to think about liquidity. They want to be building a product that will bring in the most money. This process works well in primary markets, or proven secondary markets, where buyers are plentiful.

Smaller markets are also great places to build in. Land is cheaper, with little or no development charges. Municipalities are usually supportive, meaning a project can get going quickly. Rents are surprisingly strong in these markets, but liquidity is going to be lower, which is not a big problem if the plan is to be a long-term keeper. For those wishing to sell, it's still salable, but the number of offers will be lower than in larger markets.

What's Most Affected

	IF SELLING	IF KEEPING
Business Model	Build for a quick profit and move on	Focus is on long-term wealth creation
Where to Build	Primary and proven secondary markets—selling is more difficult in tertiary markets. Consider markets that are more active.	Primary and secondary, though many smaller tertiary markets are great for long-term holding
Lobby	Less impressive but functional	An impressive lobby for a great arrival experience
Materials & Finish	Condo spec	Durable and long-lasting
Amenities	Lobby lounge, a fitness center, a party room, and storage for incoming packages. For larger buildings—a yoga studio, theater, conference room, and a dog run and pet wash with separate entrance	Lobby lounge, a fitness center, a party room, and storage for incoming packages. For larger buildings—a yoga studio, theater, conference room, and a dog run and pet wash with separate entrance
Occupancy Date	At the beginning of peak-leasing season to most lease quickly	Though leasing season is important, a developer will have more time to lease properly
Rent Setting	Vital to achieve highest rents immediately	Rent shortfalls can be made up upon re-leasing due to turnover
Leasing Focus	Highest rents as a priority	Highest rents but with more time to achieve them
Property Management	Bring us in, lease it up, and hire a third-party manager to shovel the snow and collect the rent	Consider creating a property management division. Learn the lease-up business well so it becomes a core competency.
Financing	Small percentage of initial equity, borrow the remainder to build. On selling, pay off loans and partners, split the profits. Let the buyer finance the sale.	Initial equity is higher. Pay off construction loan via a take-out mortgage.
When Sold	The active leasing reaches ~ 75 percent	Not sold—held. However, selling after a time is possible.
Capital Gains	Approx. of profit is 50 percent tax free. Remainder taxed at just over 50 percent.	None until the building is sold
Long-term Planning	Long-term wealth generation is dependent on profits invested in other instruments. Intergenerational wealth is not dependent on managing built buildings.	Long-term wealth generation is ongoing and managed by a family office with a focus to provide long-term wealth creation and continuity.

Figure 13.2 - Keep or Sell Impact

Please contact **Rock Advisors** for details on all of the above. The differences may change based on the developer's situation, local requirements, tax regulations, or other factors.

What Is Not Affected

Not everything is directly affected by the hold-sell decision. The two largest expenses during and after construction are municipal taxes and utility costs. They account for more than half of a building's expenses. Since NOI determines the building's value, it makes sense to lower these two regardless of whether building to keep or to sell.

Once a building is leased-up, or in the process of leasing, a developer can probably sell the building fairly easily if the market is good. This allows them to sell early without a big hit to the cap rate or the actual price.

Property Management

To maintain its attractiveness to renters and continue to be financially successful, an apartment building needs a competent property management system in place.

If a merchant developer is building one apartment, it may make sense to bring us in, lease it up, and hire a third-party manager to shovel the snow and collect the rent. But if a developer is planning to hold properties for a long period of time, they should consider creating a property management division. Learn the lease-up business well so it then becomes part of the business's core competency.

When To Hold / When To Sell

The Merchant Builder

Pre-sale Period

During the pre-sale period—which means the builder owns a piece of land, some renderings, and little else but a dream—no one is going to buy. Institutional buyers will not buy a lot (just land), a vision, and pay a price based on future income, future expenses, and future cap rates. Too many of those factors are not controllable. The reason buyers pay very low cap rates for apartments is that they want stability and a steady income. At the beginning of the process, the "money machine" is not there yet.

If the builder does have a site that's fully entitled, and they've got an approved site plan, then they could sell the land. However, they're not selling the apartment building on that land even though that land may be worth more because of the approval to build.

Is it possible to forward sell a full building? Yes, and there will be lots of buyers for that.

During Construction

A building can be sold during construction—the further along, the better. Just be aware that it will be a delicate negotiation. We've done a number of these and we know how to make this work, but it's complex. A builder won't leave a lot of money on the table if they do it at the right time and do it properly.

During Lease-up / After Stabilization

The real money can be made once the building is built. However, the rental income is not yet established, and we all know from previous chapters that the value of the building depends on the rental income. Lease-up can now begin. Our recommendation is not to sell the building empty as no buyer will pay full price.

> *Our job is to get a developer from the building concept at the very beginning to a stabilized building where it will have achieved maximum value.*

The real money is made at lease-up. A building can be sold during lease-up, with greater confidence in income potential as the percentage of leased units grows. As more and more of the building is leased, a developer can expect greater and greater returns. It can also be sold when fully stabilized. Ideally, one year's worth of stabilized income allows the buyer to be very confident in what they're buying and the seller confident in what they're selling. Selling at this stage is the typical selling strategy employed by new merchant builders who have limited market exposure. By first building then leasing a property, they give potential buyers the confidence that the rents achieved are sustainable and the building is of an appropriate level of quality.

Once a builder's first building is completed and their reputation is solidified, they can begin requesting concessions and potentially move up the date of sale into the period of construction, or in the event of a strong relationship between buyer and seller, move up the sale during pre-construction. Only with sufficient confidence in both the process and the developer will a buyer consider purchasing a property in its earliest stages.

What Determines the Selling Price?

The market determines the price of the building. A broker who understands the marketplace and who widely exposes a building to potential buyers will secure the highest price. More offers are always a win for the developer. The developer should never just take the first offer that comes along, potentially leaving millions on the table. Not every buyer wants to pay the higher prices new buildings command. A new building is a core holding, one that will produce steady income for the long term, both cash flow and capital gains.

Most building costs cannot be controlled. Land is bought at market price, the building is built at market prices, operating costs are what they are, and the market determines the cap rate. What's left is rent—a variable within a developer's control. As discussed in Chapter 11, "The Four Factors That Drive Rent," getting the rents as high as possible is a developer's primary focus.

When a building is sold, the major expense will be the taxes owing. Our company spends a significant amount of time on minimizing those taxes. That tax bill should be thought about from the earliest stages in order to keep it as low as possible.

Summary

A developer is better off selling a stabilized building than selling an empty building, with leasing beginning well before the Certificate of Occupancy date, which in effect, is the day they begin constructing the building. The building's price is then determined by the rental rates of the units.

Keeping the Building

Hold Forever

Holding forever is a wonderful option for a developer and their family. It gives them plenty of flexibility for the future, leaving the option to sell later if goals change or good opportunities arise.

Conclusion

Without knowing whether a building will be sold or kept, it cannot be designed or positioned to achieve its maximum value. Without this decision made early in the project, a developer will not realize the full potential value of the project. Before any building is built, the long-term goals for that structure need to be established. Those goals also have implications for the developer's long-term business plans, which include how the business will be maintained by future generations.

Kanata Lakes—William's Court: A Sales Story

Challenge

The William's Court at Kanata Lakes development was, at the time, the largest new apartment transaction in Canadian history. The project was the largest purpose-built multifamily housing development to be built in 40 years.

Long before its conception, the developer, Francis Lépine, became fascinated with apartment building when, as a young man, he was sweeping out the Olympic Village in Montreal. His father, René Lépine, long considered the largest and most influential developer in Quebec, gave Francis the opportunity to realize his own apartment-development dreams.

Though now successful in his own right, Francis yearned for a pioneering project to fulfill his own visions. This turned out to be the William's Court at Kanata Lakes project. However, due to the massive scale of the development—741 units spread over four buildings—it required capital that most developers couldn't get access to.

The solution was to build the buildings in phases and develop a joint venture partnership with the commitment to buy the buildings as they were being built, thus providing capital for the next phase.

Action

To complement Lépine's vision, we needed buyers who shared in that vision. To make this work, trust and transparency was essential between the parties over the seven years needed to complete this project.

We assembled a group of buyers, the lead being Killam Apartment REIT, and two investors: Kuwait Finance House (KFH) and AIMCo. The first two buildings, A and B, were then sold. Unexpectedly, KFH exited the deal, leaving the project underfunded. However, the value proposition and opportunity available enabled us to bring in KingSett Capital to fill the gap.

When Building B began to lease, Building A had already stabilized, with up to 30 percent of its apartments turning over. Thus, the buildings were in direct competition.

We also knew that when Building C, then D, became available to occupy, the same scenario would repeat, and with an even greater level of competition. We had to do something to minimize the consequences.

Part one of our solution was to sell Building A to Killam Apartment REIT—and have them manage it as well—while Francis Lépine continued to lease Building B. Part two was to have all stakeholders agree to maintain rent consistency to lessen competition within the community.

Result

In brokering the forward sales of these four buildings with multiple entities, it was agreed that no written agreement could anticipate all the issues that could possibly arise over its seven-year lifespan. Thus, we got the parties to agree to remain flexible and be willing to come together when an unanticipated situation arose to hammer out a solution. The aim was to keep the project on course while still satisfying each group's core investment goals.

The agreement turned out to be relatively short, especially for a project of this magnitude. But the parties knew that challenges could be successfully met and solved as a single entity. When issues did surface, they were quickly dealt with so the project could move forward as intended.

Also, to cement his reputation as a trusted and competent developer, Francis Lépine actually included attractive features in Building B—ones not present in Building A—thus proving to the investors that their commitment to buy Buildings C and D was not misplaced. As a result, the sale of those two buildings went very smoothly as trust had been established between buyer and seller.

Testimonial: Francis Lépine, Lépine Corporation

 Derek, known as a broker by profession, is much more than that.

Firstly, his core competency of making a deal work and his ability to create and maintain trusting relationships between partners is exceptional. He's not going to come into a deal and go home when it's done. Working with him is an ongoing relationship—and a rewarding one.

He and I have had a 20-year relationship. When we've worked together, his desire and commitment for open communication between parties has amazed me, as has his ability to structure deals creatively and fairly. Those exceptional abilities keep relationships functional and productive, fostering trust and letting the buyer and seller work together profitably and amicably.

Secondly, he has a quality that I admire—which is his passion for teaching and communicating with others. This truly sets him apart. Up-and-coming builders and property owners will profit by just listening to his ideas and reflecting on how those ideas can be of value to their own businesses.

We also share a common expectation: to pass on our knowledge and have the next generations outperform us.

Go Canada Go!

Francis Lépine and Derek Lobo viewing the site model

Ariel view of the site

Figure 13.3 - Kanata Lakes - Williams Court

Intergenerational Wealth

Introduction

We think it's every parent's dream to have their children come into their business.

During the course of a developer's lifetime, a great deal of wealth is created. Where that accumulated wealth and ongoing cash flow goes, and how it's managed after the original developer is no longer active, must be planned for well in advance. This ensures that surviving family members and future generations enjoy the benefits of that wealth without the strife caused by inadequate or poor planning.

Considerations:
- Continuation of family control of the company
- Wealth transfer, preservation, and growth
- Protection of future generations' lifestyles
- Philanthropy to support causes that are meaningful
- Family unity

What does this have to do with building apartments? Well, nothing, or quite a bit. It's really about life and the value created, and thinking about a developer's family legacy. It's essential to begin thinking about this now and not when conditions make decision-making difficult.

A Transition Process Is Essential

Apartments are the best way for a real estate family to transition their wealth from one generation to another.

Over the last half century, real estate has helped create significant wealth for what are now second- and third-generation families and their partners. In many instances, the initial builders or founders have left behind significant real estate holdings to their heirs. If they haven't, they may soon do so. Those assets produce an ongoing cash flow legacy of many buildings of different value, and for families with as many as five, 10 or 15 heirs.

Begin projects with the future in mind.

Developers, though focused on the projects at hand, must decide how and by whom those apartments will be managed far into the future. The tendency to delay these decisions will prevent future issues. In essence, the decisions made now are larger than any one building, encompassing the future of the wealth it generates and how it's distributed or managed. Good, sound advice at the earliest stages can save a developer's family needless grief and turmoil and save countless dollars over time. Our experience in these matters can supply the wisdom needed for obvious future issues as well as those issues that may not be so obvious to younger developers.

How Should That Process Be Organized and Maintained?

Our Solution

Over the years, we have developed an exclusive process based on our unique experience, knowledge, and skills to best serve families in situations like these. We are not a typical brokerage firm using worn-out conventional processes that only work when conditions are ideal. Rather, we are a dynamic team of innovators with the goal of creating real value for our clients. We have a proven track record, working closely with many families and real estate portfolios for more than 25 years. We know how to efficiently and effectively deal with differing and complex family situations and provide a wide range of consulting services as well as brokerage services, if ultimately required.

We know that when families embark on this journey without an external facilitator, they will see slow progress and duplicated work, both the result of poor communication and lack of management. Our aim is to make the process more collaborative and transparent wherever possible. When a stalemate occurs, owners may not be able to decide how to best move forward. We provide leadership and help find the "bold moves to get the process going." Ideally, we move forward with full consensus, and when one party cannot find common ground, we can. In this situation it would be an inverted process that can still lead to a positive outcome, but it is more complex to execute. An overview is included on the next page (Figure 14.1). Though we have successfully executed deals with this process, it is just one of many processes available.

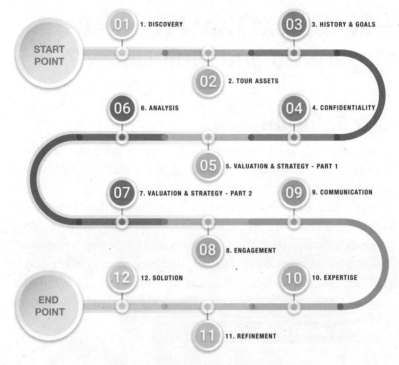

Figure 14.1 - Example Solution Process

As one of the most connected teams in the real estate industry nationwide, we have built a network of trusted relationships that allows us to better serve developers in all circumstances. We have the experience and unique qualifications to handle complex ownership situations. We understand that this is a long-term process that requires out-of-the-box thinking. When dealing with a challenging scenario, results rarely take less than a year.

We Stay in Touch

Over the years, our services have evolved and grown. Clients with whom we have consulted for in different capacities now come to us directly or indirectly, knowing we can help them resolve tense situations professionally and objectively.

We value transparency through the process, from objectives and solution methods, to how long the process will take. We also maintain a high level of neutrality in order that family members know that everyone's needs and feelings are equally considered. In some cases, neutrality is almost impossible (see process in Figure 14.1), but the process is still executed. We can successfully manage both scenarios.

Risks

As time goes on, family businesses face risks.

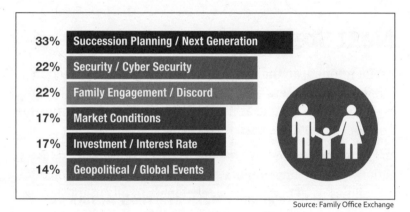

Source: Family Office Exchange

Figure 14.2 - Risks Families Face

Challenges Grow with Each Generation

Every family is unique. However, there are predictable trends and perspectives that naturally arise in family-owned portfolios. As families grow over the generations, goals easily achieved during the early generations may not always be shared, resulting in greater challenges for families arriving at a consensus. First-generation members who had hoped to provide a steady livelihood for their children and grandchildren may not have anticipated the growth of their portfolios, nor the inherent complexities that might arise.

Don't Leave Potential Issues for Others to Solve

Putting a structure in place now to handle the family business is the greatest gift a developer can bestow on their heirs. Developers who invest the time to consider their current situation and options at an early stage means tomorrow's challenges are far less likely to be disruptive.

Next Steps

As mentioned at the outset of this chapter, this section is all about awareness and preparation. Our hope is that it is insightful and beneficial. Remember, an investment in time now will smooth the road forward.

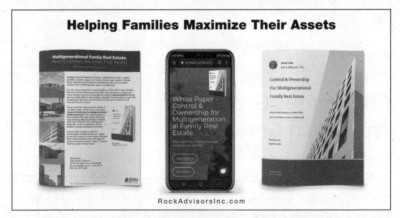

Figure 14.3 - Multigenerational Family Real Estate

Regardless of the developer's current situation or goals, we're always here as a solution provider to help manage the transition of control and ongoing ownership of their real estate assets.

Conclusion

The "why" behind building apartments always comes back to the family. It's about wealth preservation, tax deferral, and cash flow. And the reason this all works is that rentals really are the best way for a real estate family to transition wealth from one generation to another.

The subject of multigenerational family real estate may not be forefront in a developer's mind today, but now is the best time to solve potential future conflicts. Most likely, there will be topics they're not currently aware of.

> *Our message to you: wisdom is often learned from one's mistakes, but wisdom can also be learned from the mistakes of others.*

Our team is uniquely connected to industry experts, with an established record of working with real estate families. We have helped them solve countless difficult multigenerational challenges—let us know how we can help you.

> *LESSON:*
> *Rental apartments are the best way for a real estate family to transition wealth from one generation to another. Planning ahead for a smooth transition between generations is how developers avoid unnecessary challenges for their future heirs.*

Figure 14.4 - Multigenerational Family Portfolio

Epilogue

●

For the developer seeking both short-term capital gains and longer-term wealth creation, there's no doubt that multifamily development is the best opportunity for any asset class. Current economic conditions only serve to strengthen the developer's position. By combining their existing skills with the guidelines, advice, and processes described in this book, they stand to build products that meet or exceed marketplace needs, giving them a calculated advantage in the industry.

> *We champion the "hero developer," the one who risks everything to build a vision into a successful apartment and opens up an opportunity for a great portfolio.*

We want to present developers as apartment scientists, with our team of advisors taking care of the details, freeing them to focus on building a business that programmatically builds successful rental apartments time and time again.

Over the years, it's become obvious that the "why" behind building apartments always comes back to the family. It's about wealth preservation, tax deferral, and cash flow. The reason this all works is that rentals really are the best way for a real estate family to transition wealth from one generation to another. The significant wealth that developers create inevitably gets passed down through the generations. Managing that wealth takes organization, structure, and a family enterprise following a set of guidelines designed to sustain or grow that wealth as well as being mindful of family dynamics.

Although the preceding chapters contain a wealth of information, they only scratch the surface. Intentional apartment development is a process. We continue to be on a journey to enable apartment scientists to be the best they can be. Our appreciation of the complete project cycle, relationships, vision, technology, timely factors, development of business tools, and focused thought leadership is what we'll continue to execute with intention.

It is our hope that the end result for the reader is to become *The Intentional Apartment Developer*, one who leverages the available knowledge and expertise and continues to grow their vision for a bright future!

My Notes

My Notes

My Notes

My Notes

My Notes

My Notes